The Stroll

A Stroll Through the Bible

With **Dr. J. Stanley McQuade**
Art by Patty Ludwig Jung

© 2017

Published in the United States by Nurturing Faith Inc., Macon GA,

www.nurturingfaith.net.

Library of Congress Cataloging-in-Publication Data is available.

ISBN 978-1-63528-019-7

Cover photo by David Cassady, Faithlab. "Olive and almond trees in Nazareth."

Contents

A Stroll Through the Bible

Introduction

When I was growing up, it was difficult to avoid acquiring some knowledge of the Bible. Even if one did not attend Sunday school, it was built into the educational system and even into literature and everyday life. But all that has changed. Generations of children are growing up with little or no knowledge of the Bible. Sunday school has also changed. When we went to Sunday school every week, we learned Bible stories and even recited important passages. There was even a Sunday school exam! In order to become a Methodist minister in my day, it was necessary to pass an incredibly detailed exam in English Bible. But all that has changed too.

The authorized version of the Bible has been replaced by countless modern versions. While these contemporary versions are helpful, it seems nobody can quote scriptures from memory anymore. Current Sunday school educators feel more pressure to focus on creating a happy and meaningful experience rather than getting into the Bible. A large number of people who would have no hesitation in calling themselves Christians (and I believe them) would not do well answering even elementary questions about the Bible. They might want to read the Bible, but it is foreign to them, so they often give up after one or two attempts.

This series of stories is aimed at helping these adults and young people who would like to read and love the Bible but somehow have never managed to get into it. My plan is to stroll through the Bible, one story or passage at a time, and invite others to join me. Sooner or later in the process, if we are listening with our heart and seeking to order our lives by it, the penny drops and we are no longer getting into the Bible; the Bible is getting into us.

The basic plan of the book is to take a passage or a story from the Bible and add brief comments on it to explain it and generally to show how it may be related to our present life and circumstances. Where possible, the text of the Bible is used, but when this would take up too much space, I have summarized the text or retold the story in my own words. Patty Jung, our artist, has added drawings to bring out the meaning of the story or passage, which helps to focus the mind on the central meaning of the materials.

Studying the Bible: Moses's Method

Deuteronomy 6:4-9

Hear, O Israel: The LORD our God, the LORD is one.[a] Love the LORD your God with all your heart and with all your soul and with all your strength. These commandments that I give you today are to be on your hearts. Impress them on your children. Talk about them when you sit at home and when you walk along the road, when you lie down and when you get up. Tie them as symbols on your hands and bind them on your foreheads. Write them on the doorframes of your houses and on your gates.

Comment

1 Later Jews took Moses's words literally and provided little boxes (phylacteries) containing quotations from the Law, especially the *Shema* (meaning "hear," i.e., the first line from the Law cited above), which were tied upon their forehead and strapped on their right forearm. Devout Jews in Jesus's time commonly wore phylacteries. Indeed, their outlines in blood on the forearm and forehead of the figure in the shroud of Turin can be seen in detailed photographs. There can be little doubt, however, that what Moses really intended was that the Law of God should be embedded in their minds and in their actions and in their homes. And this is our business today. There is a great dearth of knowledge of the Bible among adult Christians today. Previous generations, as I mentioned already, learned the Bible stories in Sunday school and were encouraged to memorize important passages and even show their knowledge in annual exams. Sadly, much of this is gone. More up-to-date theories of education stressing enjoyment and appreciation of the Bible materials have taken over. These no doubt have their point, but they have created a vagueness in the general understanding of the Bible. Adult Christians, especially those just getting started in the faith, try to study the Bible, but they commonly find it hard going, for the Bible is a large and complex book. They do not know where to start and often become discouraged. I have come across this problem among my own friends and family, and this series of articles is what I propose to do about it.

2 We have two problems here. The first is to enable people with no familiarity with the Bible to get into it. The second and larger problem is to get the Bible into us so that it becomes part and parcel of who we are, enriching our understanding of God, becoming the furniture of our minds and steering and guiding us in our homes and lives generally.

3 I propose to deal with this problem in this series in two ways: (a) by presenting the Bible, teaching it through stories and favorite passages such as we used to learn in Sunday school; and (b) by making comments on these stories and passages, designed to show how they apply in our lives in the present world.

4 So let's go to it, read it, learn it, think about it, and apply it in our everyday living until it becomes incorporated into our very bones. For it is God's principal way of communicating with us and teaching us how he wants us to live and what he wants us to do.

Part 1

Old Testament

The Creation

Genesis 1

In the beginning God created the heavens and the earth. Now the earth was formless and empty, darkness was over the surface of the deep, and the Spirit of God was hovering over the waters.

And God said, "Let there be light," and there was light. God saw that the light was good, and he separated the light from the darkness. God called the light "day," and the darkness he called "night." And there was evening, and there was morning—the first day. (vv. 1-5)

Read through verse 25 in your Bible.

Comment

1 This ancient picture of the creation in the book of Genesis is not intended to teach us science. If Genesis had been written in terms of modern science, the ancients would not have known what God was talking about. Indeed, if Genesis was written as currently portrayed to us by astrophysicists, we ourselves would have difficulty knowing what it was saying. The old couplet has it that "Nature and Nature's laws lay bathed in night / God said 'Let Newton be' and all was light." But a later reply to this runs, "But not for long, the Devil howling 'Ho! Let Einstein be' restored the status quo."

The biblical cosmology is not describing how things really are, but how they would have looked to the eyes of the ancients. It is also how we would see the world if we had not been to school and learned about more up-to-date science. And from this perspective it is apt. Our world may not be a bowl hanging upside down over a floating plate, but that is what it looks like to the innocent eye. The heavenly bodies are located in it to provide light and for all sorts of other purposes, and the rain leaks down through it. The earth then appears like a plate floating on the waters beneath, which surround it with the seas and surge up through it in fountains and rivers and lakes. This simple descriptive picture can be filled out by any scientific knowledge we may possess. It even has a time dimension. It did not appear all at once. This picture had to be expanded when Galileo and Copernicus and the like used the information provided by the telescope to show that the earth revolved around the sun, not vice versa. Who knows what the next version of the universe will be or how we will need to modify our notions about it? But no matter what view of the cosmos may be current, this simple picture can be expanded to encompass it.

2. And what does the creation account of Genesis tell us?
   - That God created the world. It did not arise by happenstance but was the product of an infinitely powerful mind.[1] To hold otherwise is not only statistically unlikely;[2] it is positively unimaginable. It is like thinking that a lightning bolt striking a rubbish heap could produce a Boeing 727.
   - That it is wonderful. To behold it, to study it, is to delight in it, to marvel at its intricate systems and arrangements.
   - That it is awesomely beautiful. With mountains, seas, forests, colors, and the vast work force of living creatures that keep it running, all the intricate arrangements delight the eye and dazzle the mind.
   - That we are in charge of it. We are to enjoy it, care for it, maintain it, and use it responsibly.

3. With God in the picture, the universe is inspiring and delightful. As a chance happening it is nothing special. An agnostic once asked me what difference it made whether God existed or not. I had trouble answering the question not because there isn't an answer but rather because the difference is so enormous. It is like asking a happily married person what they think about marriage. Without God in the picture, the universe is just a great accidental machine. The beauty and wonder of it do not point in that direction and can only be appreciated as the garden of Eden portrays it: the handiwork of God put there for our welfare and our pleasure, ordinary and intellectual. To look out the window and not to see the little birds and the flowers and the trees and everything else as the handiwork of the almighty creator is to miss a lot. The Genesis account also provides us with the only satisfactory reason for our duty to care for our world. If it is just an accident, so what?

4. I realize that we must also consider other aspects of our world that are not obviously benign. That is the great topic of the book of Job, and we will talk more about that later. In the meantime consider whether we would be better off in a world where everything was hunky-dory, all sweetness and light.

---

[1] Until recently, the dominant view was that matter had always been there. The "big bang" theory is more in line with the biblical account that God created our universe out of nothing.

[2] See *The Philosophical Scientists* by David Foster for probability studies exploding the view that a million monkeys tapping randomly on typewriters could eventually produce the complete works of Shakespeare.

The Garden of Eden

Genesis 2

Now the LORD God had planted a garden in the east, in Eden; and there he put the man he had formed. The LORD God made all kinds of trees grow out of the ground—trees that were pleasing to the eye and good for food. In the middle of the garden were the tree of life and the tree of the knowledge of good and evil. A river watering the garden flowed from Eden; from there it was separated into four headwaters.... The LORD God took the man and put him in the Garden of Eden to work it and take care of it. (vv. 8-10, 15)

Comment

1 The garden mentioned here is not like the garden in the front (or back) yard of our houses, but a pleasure park, a great estate like those set up for the enjoyment of the great Persian kings in which they hunted and generally had a good time. The name *Eden* seems to be related to the Aramaic word for "fruitful"

or "wellness" or "watered." The river flowing out of it is said to divide into four heads. Two of these, the Tigris and the Euphrates, are well known to us. The other two are not easily identified. They were said by the Jewish historian Josephus to be the Nile and the Ganges, but who knows? The tree of knowledge of good and evil is not representing the ability to know when things are good or bad, which would be a good thing, something to be truly desired. It is rather about determining or deciding for ourselves what is good and what is evil, putting ourselves in the place of God. Identifying the tree of life is a more difficult matter. One view is that it is the same as the tree of knowledge of good and evil, which is hardly likely. Another is that it could provide everlasting life such as is possessed by God. Whether man was intended to eat of this and live forever is questionable but held by some. In the New Testament the tree of life is linked with the eternal life of heaven and those who attain to it (Rev 22), a more likely idea.

2 Man is put into the garden to dress it and care for it. We are obviously meant to enjoy it too, for the trees are pleasant to the eye and good for food. But we are also in charge of its maintenance and welfare, to dress it and care for it, like a gardener. We are expected to share the task with God, so we are held responsible for its good condition.

3 What is dressing? It seems to imply more than just weeding. Development of some kind is intended. It can therefore be taken as a proper development of the earth to meet human needs while preserving its wonderful character. This of course raises many questions about what is proper and permissible development and what is destructive—and how the balance between them is to be struck. There are often two sides to every beneficial advance in the management of natural resources. Hydroelectric power provided energy that has transformed society, providing clean fuel, heating and light, power for domestic utilities such as refrigeration and preparation of food. It is indeed a watershed between more primitive existence and modern life. But it has its downside too. Mighty rivers that used to reach the sea now end up absorbed into the ground, and numerous important fish such as salmon can no longer get beyond the dams to spawn, so fish populations are becoming seriously depleted. We need to look for ways in which we can eat our cake and still have it. Providing pathways for the fish past the dams is one solution, and opening up the dams at spawning times is another. These would preserve the new uses of water without affecting the environment any more than is necessary. The use of atomic energy is another difficult issue. Russia and

China, desperate for cheap energy, are going ahead with atomic energy systems despite their problems (getting rid of the atomic waste is one; nuclear meltdowns are another). Fossil fuels are the least expensive and obvious choice as an energy source, but carbon emissions are one problem, oil spills another.

4 This raises the question of environmentalism generally, the proper use of the world's resources. Destruction of the environment was well advanced in Roman times (especially deforestation), but it was not noticed. Environmental values were not included by St. Thomas Aquinas in his list of the great principles of natural law. The environment and its resources seemed too vast to be affected by anything we might do. But with increases in the human population and advances in technology, this has changed. Huge expanses of water, even oceans, have become polluted. All sorts of animals, birds, fish, and insects are becoming extinct, even on a daily basis, due to pollution or destruction of their environments or overfishing or illegal hunting. Medical researchers are complaining that poisonous insects and snakes, so useful in the creation of desperately needed medicines, are becoming harder to find. Conflict between commercial and environmental interests is very much with us (undersea oil exploration and fracking for example). What is the right balance is a good question. But what is undeniable is that there should be a balance. We are entrusted with the stewardship of the world.

5 The creation of the world for pleasure and enjoyment is another aspect of the garden. A paradise, as mentioned earlier, was a pleasure park where the great people played and generally enjoyed themselves. Beauty is another important aspect of the story. The trees not only provided food but were pleasing to the eye—beautiful. Many of the delightful colors of plants and birds and other creatures have functional uses, but they are also lovely to behold. The way in which they fit together in the great working system of nature is also marvelous. God could have simplified the system using machines that produced three meals a day and cleared up the mess every evening. But he chose to provide the great biosystems, self-maintaining and self-repairing, as we untangle them and seek to understand them.

6 I was once asked by a secular Jew what difference it would make if God did not exist. The question is difficult, not so much because there are no differences but because there are so many that we do not know where to start. I am sorry for people whose outlook on life and the world does not include the Creator. They miss so much. To look out in the morning on the trees and the flowers and the birds and the butterflies and only see them as pawns in the great struggle for

survival is a barren and uninspiring sight. To see them as a wonderful, extremely complex way of carrying out the business of the world is interesting and inspiring as well as being awesomely beautiful. And it should inspire us to wish to maintain it and avoid spoiling it. There is no sound foundation for environmentalism other than the story of the garden. What does it matter if the landscape is ruined or bothersome species disappear? We will not be around long enough to know about it, and why should we care for future generations if we have no responsibility for nature? Our children will just have to learn to put up with it if they are still here.

There is a lot to think about in the story of the garden of Eden. It is a powerful set of spectacles through which to look on life and the world. The great Swiss theologian Emil Brunner has commented that he will not bother to have a serious conversation about important topics about life and living with anyone who has not read and thought about the stories in the earlier part of Genesis. Their views, he says, are bound to be superficial.

The Creation of Man

Genesis 1–2

Then God said, "Let us make mankind in our image, in our likeness, so that they may rule over the fish in the sea and the birds in the sky, over the livestock and all the wild animals,[a] and over all the creatures that move along the ground." So God created mankind in his own image, in the image of God he created them; male and female he created them. (1:26-27)

Then the LORD God formed a man[c] from the dust of the ground and breathed into his nostrils the breath of life, and the man became a living being. (2:7)

Comment

1 There are two accounts in Genesis of the creation of man. The one in Genesis 1 is a plain statement that God created man in his own image and likeness and gave man dominion over the whole earth and everything in it. The Hebrew word used here for man is *Adam* (from *adamah*, meaning "the earth"), and it is made clear that this is a generic designation, including both male and female. The second account in Genesis 2 is a more poetic account where God made a man from the dust of the earth and breathed into his nostrils the breath of life. God then placed him in the garden of Eden to enjoy it and care for it. Eve was made later from a rib taken out of man while he was in a deep sleep.

2 What is the image and likeness of God? Obviously it does not intend the infinite properties of God: infinite knowledge, infinite power, and infinite goodness. But man, though having many things in common with animals, has a few divine extras as well, which resemble important aspects of God. Man is creative, appreciates beauty, has a sense of right and wrong, and above all seeks fellowship. And the Genesis story makes it clear that man, like God, has the freedom to make choices of all kinds, including moral ones, and has also the ability to think about and understand the creation. We know intuitively that we possess these capacities, and they are not explained by secular accounts of creation that leave God out of the picture. This notion of the image of God differs markedly from all the godless descriptions of man. The Marxist idea is that man's life is determined by economic factors. Freud's idea is that man is driven by powerful subconscious factors that become molded into behavioral patterns. Man has also

been described as a tool-using creature and by other secular modes of thinking. None of these sufficiently explains human beings as we know them. The more recent existentialist pictures of man are equally superficial. Reinhold Niebuhr's criticisms of secular descriptions of man in his *The Nature and Destiny of Man* are obviously valid. The Genesis account of mankind sets the standard for any account of human nature. The worst human beings know the difference between right and wrong, and the most depraved and warped specimens of humanity have some measure of creativity, a notion of the value of truth, and a sense, however primitive, of the beauty of things.

3 Having freedom of choice, an important part of the image and likeness of God, also carries with it the capacity to sin. One might think it would have been better if the Creator had made mankind so subservient to himself that they could not, or were afraid to, sin. But this would be to make man not a person but a machine. God wished to have companions, and this required something in common between man and his creator. We find in the Genesis story that God walked and conversed with Adam and Eve in the garden in the cool of the evening, the normal time for socializing in the hot climate of the Middle East. God wants to share life with us.

4 And mankind is made a social being, with the basic unit of the family and, beyond that, the various tribes and nations and social arrangements of humanity. This provision is obviously good, providing beneficial connections between people and the possibility of extending and increasing those good things from one social group to another and from one generation to the next. But there is the great risk too of the system becoming warped and distorted and passing on evil traditions and institutions from population to population and from one generation to another. This dangerous process is described in the Genesis story, from the first murder to the cities of the plain where evil was standard, everyday behavior.

5 God responds in Genesis to this evil warping of creation by judgment, wiping out the cities of the plain and even the great mass of mankind in the flood. But the positive response of God was to call Abraham and establish the family and generation of those who followed God. In this extended family all the nations of the earth were to be blessed and find salvation. This story will be taken up later.

The Creation of Woman

Genesis 2:18-24

The LORD God said, "It is not good for the man to be alone. I will make a help-er suitable for him."… So the LORD God caused the man to fall into a deep sleep; and while he was sleeping, he took one of the man's ribs[g] and then closed up the place with flesh. Then the LORD God made a woman from the rib[h] he had taken out of the man, and he brought her to the man. The man said, "This is now bone of my bones and flesh of my flesh; she shall be called 'woman,' for she was taken out of man." That is why a man leaves his father and mother and is united to his wife, and they become one flesh. (vv. 18, 21-24)

Comment

1 Jokingly, this has been called the first surgery under general anesthesia in history, and skeptics used to point out that there is no missing rib in men. This was countered by pointing out that provided the periosteum is left intact, the rib will regrow. But what is the point in this story? Why the rib? Obviously, as is made clear in the concluding sentence, it has something to do with the intimacy of the relationship of man and woman in marriage. They belong to one another, and each is incomplete without the other.

2 Jesus cited this story in response to the Sadducees' superficial views of marriage and divorce. In the Bible the two become one flesh (one body) in marriage. This "one flesh" doctrine is particularly important in relation to the question of who is the boss in a marriage. The official answer is that the man is the head of the woman. But the question is made irrelevant so far as Christians are concerned when we consider that the two are united in one person. As St. Paul comments, no one hates his own flesh but cherishes it (Eph 5:29). Decisions must be made together. If one party is strongly opposed on an issue, either they must be persuaded or some compromise needs to be sought and reached.

3 I think we must accept that so far as the Bible is concerned, the husband is normally the CEO of the marriage business and, as in dancing, most women expect the man to lead. But as management consultants are quick to point out, the dictatorial model of management is not effective. St. Paul, a strong advocate of the place of man in marriage, is quick to dissociate himself and the Bible view from this kind of male dominance.

4 It is also clear both in the Bible and in literature that the woman can be the wiser and the stronger partner. Priscilla is always mentioned in the New Testament along with her husband Aquila, and from time to time ahead of him. Dickens, in his novel *Bleak House*, features a retired soldier with a wise and strong wife. When people come to him with problems, seeking advice, he always says to his wife, "Old girl, tell them my opinion," adding under his breath, "Discipline must be preserved." Many a minister's services have been enhanced by such a wife. I could provide dozens of examples without any trouble, and any man who feels threatened by a talented wife has something wrong with him. Each partner brings to the marriage whatever gifts they have, and they should work together with gratitude.

5 What is the difference between a man and a woman, between male and female? This question superficially is so obvious as to be almost silly. But other than the outward physical appearance, what is the difference? Or rather what are the differences? Why the fetus develops one way or the other depends on the production of the male or female hormone, testosterone or estrogen, but the difference between these two is a single hydrogen atom. However, the personality changes that follow from this tiny chemical variation are enormous. It is not just physical; it profoundly affects personality. This can be seen even in children: the girls like to play with dolls and the boys with weapons. These are only generalizations of course, but generally they hold. This difference, subtle though it may be, is familiar to every church pastor. Where would the church be without women? Jews wisely trace their descent through their mother, and it is notable in the book of Kings that the first thing noted about a king was his mother. In a reported lecture, the speaker was pointing out the very slight difference between male and female hormones when someone jumped up at the back and shouted, "Thank God for the difference!" To this we say "Amen" and bless God for his infinite wisdom. In my lifetime the effect of gender difference on choice of profession has drastically changed. Many jobs and professions formerly considered exclusively male occupations are now also open to women. Certain branches of surgery, for instance, were more or less closed for most women because physical strength was required (e.g., orthopedics). The development of technology has changed all of this. You don't need to be physically strong anymore, only adept at using mechanical or computerized instruments. The boundary separating men and women has thus tended to be blurred or nonexistent in almost all occupations and professions. The same is true in reverse. Occupations that at one time were considered to be the prerogative of women, like nursing, are now open to men as well. However, personality differences still exist and tend to affect in a subtle way the manner in which men and women function, and generally for the better.

The Arrival of Sin

Genesis 3

Now the serpent was more crafty than any of the wild animals the LORD God had made. He said to the woman, "Did God really say, 'You must not eat from any tree in the garden'?"

The woman said to the serpent, "We may eat fruit from the trees in the garden, but God did say, 'You must not eat fruit from the tree that is in the middle of the garden, and you must not touch it, or you will die.'" (vv. 1-3)

Read through verse 11 in your Bible.

Comment

1 This simple story is profoundly meaningful. It speaks of many things and describes the ultimate nature of sin. Sin is not just doing "bad things"; these are commonly the result of sin, but its root is something else. The tree of knowledge of good and evil sounds like a good thing to eat and enjoy, but what it represents is something quite different and evil. The serpent promises that if, by disobeying God's command, you take and eat of its fruit, you will be able to decide for yourself what is good and what is evil; you don't need God anymore. The nature of sin is to put oneself in the place of God, to shake off his guiding and controlling hand. It is usurpation, in effect a palace coup. It is represented in the New Testament parables as the servants taking over the vineyard, beating and abusing those sent to set them straight and eventually murdering their Lord's only son (Luke 20:9-19 et al.).

2 This story also describes the shame of sin, like being naked in public. The guilty couple fly from the presence of God (walking and conversing in the garden in the cool of the evening) and make aprons of leaves to cover their shame. Guilt is built into human nature. The most wicked know they are doing wrong (as Charles Manson admitted) and therefore feel guilt, though that will not prevent them from doing it again.

3 Their eviction from the garden describes the loss of all the good and pleasant things given to them in God's creation.

4 All the guilty parties are punished. The curse of man is hard labor to survive in a hostile world that grows thorns and thistles, labor that is endured but not enjoyed. The curse of woman is the pain and danger of childbirth and to be under the thumb of her stronger husband. The serpent is cursed with the everlasting enmity of mankind. Even the ground is cursed, for with the corruption of the steward it will no longer be properly cared for and will indeed be abused.

5 As we shall see in the succeeding chapters of Genesis, this bad beginning leads to a downward slide into more obviously evil things. The first murder follows, Cain killing his brother Abel. Overweening ambition appears, represented by the tower of Babel. And shortly after, Sodom and Gomorrah, the cities of the plain, appear, where every kind of evil and cruelty was normal and usual.

6 But the final comment must be that these curses are removed in Christ. The downward slide into ruin and destruction is replaced by an upward trend with the restoring of right relationships, beginning with the relationship to God himself. The curse of meaningless labor is transformed into enjoyable and useful occupation. A sense of worthwhileness is the secret of enjoyment of one's work, even when it is difficult. Childbirth becomes not a feared curse but joy that a child has come into the world so that all the pain is forgotten. Woman is not just the slave and plaything of man but a necessary and loved partner. Nature and the environment share in the joy of salvation, the natural surroundings being seen and treated as a wonderful gift of God. Even the serpent gets a little leg up here and there. Poisonous creatures of all kinds, threatened with extinction, are now protected because they are recognized as important in the scheme of nature and also useful in developing new treatments for serious diseases and disorders.

The Tower of Babel

Genesis 11

Now the whole world had one language and a common speech. As people moved eastward, they found a plain in Shinar and settled there.

They said to each other, "Come, let's make bricks and bake them thoroughly." They used brick instead of stone, and tar for mortar. Then they said, "Come, let us build ourselves a city, with a tower that reaches to the heavens, so that we may make a name for ourselves; otherwise we will be scattered over the face of the whole earth."

But the LORD came down to see the city and the tower the people were building. The LORD said, "If as one people speaking the same language they have begun to do this, then nothing they plan to do

will be impossible for them. Come, let us go down and confuse their language so they will not understand each other."

So the LORD scattered them from there over all the earth, and they stopped building the city. That is why it was called Babel—because there the LORD confused the language of the whole world. From there the LORD scattered them over the face of the whole earth. (vv. 1-9)

Comment

1 The plain of Shinar is mentioned in several places in the Bible. Its location is disputed, but it appears to have been somewhere in Mesopotamia. A version of this story is found elsewhere in the literature of the Middle East, and the

tower reaching to heaven may well refer to the great ziggurat in Babylon, which Alexander the Great had torn down in preparation for building an even greater one (he died before it could be built). The name *Babylon* is thus commonly linked to the idea of incomprehensible speech (babble).

2 In the Bible the story has a theological cast and concerns the pride of men wishing to make a name for themselves by establishing great empires, buildings, businesses, or even churches. The empire of Babylon was considered the epitome of human overweening ambition and wrongful pride. In the apocalypse (Revelation) the similar prideful Rome was named for Babylon (Rev 14:8).

3 This tendency to put our future reputation in the place of God's approval is universal and creeps into every human activity, even when we set out to do God's work. The little vision pops into our mind of what posterity will say about us. I am currently crafting my own memorial service (since my family insists I have one), and ever and again a little picture comes into my mind of the congregation reacting to this. It is inevitable (try to see if you can avoid it). All we can do is ask God to recall us to a better purpose and forgive our foolishness.

4 An important application of this story relates to the great empires and governments who have opposed Christ and his church. The Roman emperor Julian the Apostate planned to revive paganism to replace Christianity, but his great persecution failed. Hitler's empire was supposed to last a thousand years and collapsed in a very short time. Nikita Khrushchev was confident that Communism would bury America and rule in its place. The power of the Russian empire seemed powerful, if not invincible at the time, but rather unexpectedly it disintegrated.

5 And this is the fate of all the monuments that we erect to promote our claims to fame, small and large. Shelley wrote his poem "Ozymandias" about Pharaoh Rameses II (calling himself by his other name). Fragments of his great statue to himself (the head weighed over seven tons) were found buried in the sands of Egypt and removed to London. On the pedestal these words appear: "My name is Ozymandias, king of kings, look on my works ye mighty, and despair." But the poet notes that the image is shattered and buried in the sands and Rameses' greatness is forgotten. This is a devastating comment on human pretensions to greatness.

6 Two-term presidents of the United States are said to spend the first term getting reelected and the second term trying to promote and preserve their legacy. The same is true of people (some of them anyway) who write their memoirs.

7 Two little boys, aged four and six, the children of a Baptist minister (related to my wife Frances by marriage), were having a conversation about heaven. The younger one asked, "If I was very, very good and never did anything bad, would I get to heaven?" His brother responded, "No!" He continued, "If I got very, very rich and gave all my money to missions, would I get to heaven?" Again, the older brother said, "No!" The younger brother asked, "If I became a minister and converted everybody, would I get to heaven?" The older brother answered, "No!" Frustrated, the younger brother blurted out, "Well, what do you have to do to get to heaven?" His older brother replied, "You have to die first." The only approval worth seeking is God's, and you have to die before you can get it.

Lot's Wife:
The Danger of Looking Back

Genesis 19

The two men said to Lot, "Do you have anyone else here—sons-in-law, sons or daughters, or anyone else in the city who belongs to you? Get them out of here, because we are going to destroy this place. The outcry to the LORD against its people is so great that he has sent us to destroy it."

So Lot went out and spoke to his sons-in-law, who were pledged to marry his daughters. He said, "Hurry and get out of this place, because the LORD is about to destroy the city!"…

With the coming of dawn, the angels urged Lot, saying, "Hurry! Take your wife and your two daughters who are here, or you will be swept away when the city is punished."…

As soon as they had brought them out, one of them said, "Flee for your lives! Don't look back, and don't stop anywhere in the plain! Flee to the mountains or you will be swept away!"…

Then the LORD rained down burning sulfur on Sodom and Gomorrah—from the LORD out of the heavens. Thus he overthrew those cities and the entire plain, destroying all those living in the cities—and also the vegetation in the land. But Lot's wife looked back, and she became a pillar of salt. (vv. 12-14, 15, 17, 24-26)

Comment

1 This story tells of the ultimate depravity that comes when God is left out of the picture. The violence and sexual depravity described in his story are extreme but can be paralleled in today's societies. Such conditions carry within them the seeds of their own destruction. The wrath of God is built into the nature of things.

2 The fire from heaven described here is consistent with an explosive volcanic eruption. Lot's wife is described as lagging behind her husband, looking back with longing at the old life in the city. She could well have been enveloped in cascading salt or bitumen (later covered by salt). At any rate a pillar that looks like salt and is described as Lot's wife still resides on Mount Sodom near the Dead Sea.

3 This story has always been used to warn of the danger of looking back to the old life from which one has escaped. The Hebrew word for looking back used here is *nabat*, which means "to look on something with longing." It is a bad thing when someone has escaped from alcoholism or any other horror to start thinking back on the good things about it. In a famous Western the sheriff had just started to clean up the town when the town council started to have second thoughts and asked him to go easy. They said we know there were murders and robberies and rapes and burnings of homes and such, but other than that it wasn't such a bad place. The Israelites in the desert, after having been delivered from bondage in Egypt, looked back with longing on the sufficiency of food and water there and berated Moses for bringing them out to starve or die of thirst in the wilderness.

4 The New Testament writers constantly warn against looking back and exhort us to look forward to our good future destiny. The power of backward thinking is considerable, and it is dangerous. We can be chained and bogged down in memories of earlier wrongs or even by the memory of our former achievements (equally bad). Paul exhorts us to forget those things that are behind and to press forward to the mark of our high calling in Christ Jesus (Phil 3:13). He also advises us to focus our attention on and fill our minds with things that are just and honorable and of good report (Phil 4:8). Indeed, we need to be careful about what we allow into our minds. That which occupies our thoughts turns into our desires. We need to ask ourselves what we have been reading, watching on TV, or talking about with our friends.

5 But is there not some value in a little recreational reading, especially when we are worn out? What kind of light reading do we use, and how do we think it is valuable? The old masters of fiction had the moral and spiritual background of the Bible in general and the New Testament in particular. Much modern writing is anti-Christian and indeed immoral in tone. Often, writers include a salacious or violent episode or two, I suspect in order to boost sales. We are required to be good stewards of our time, even our leisure time.

Noah's Ark:
A Story of Judgment and Mercy

Genesis 6

The LORD saw how great the wickedness of the human race had become on the earth, and that every inclination of the thoughts of the human heart was only evil all the time. The LORD regretted that he had made human beings on the earth, and his heart was deeply troubled. So the LORD said, "I will wipe from the face of the earth the human race I have created—and with them the animals, the birds and the creatures that move along the ground—for I regret that I have made them." But Noah found favor in the eyes of the LORD.... So God said to Noah, "I am going to put an end to all people, for the earth is filled with violence because of them.... So make yourself an ark of cypress wood; make rooms in it and coat it with pitch inside and out." (vv. 5-8, 13, 14)

Comment

1 Some version of the story of the flood is found in many cultures, but in the Bible it is rewritten into theological terms as a story of sin, judgment, and salvation.

2 The ark was constructed with gopher wood, a term not otherwise found in the Bible. Its identity is contested, but the three letters of *gopher* are similar to those of *copher*, or cypress, a strong wood plentiful in the Middle East in earlier times, so cypress is the most likely material.

3 Supposedly, traces of the ark were photographed on a mountain alleged to be Mount Ararat (it is difficult to identify the precise mountain), but this entity was later found to be a normal rock formation. Indeed, there are many difficulties in taking the story literally. For instance, there are two versions, one in which

there are two creatures of every kind, another in which there are seven. How were the animals fed during the forty days afloat? Note the many rooms in the ark, presumably to keep the carnivores from devouring the rest. But what, then, did the carnivores eat? One also wonders were there two fleas or two viruses? In short, it is better to take the story as a parable (based on a real event) or, if you like, a story logic (video-clip logic). Either way, it carries a powerful message.

4 Notice the corruption of the nature of man following the rejection of God. The earth becomes filled with violence and hatred, as eventually happens in any culture when God is excluded from it. This corruption calls down God's severe reaction in judgment. And this still holds. Evil does not prosper but carries the seeds of ruin and destruction within it. Unfortunately, since we are linked together in many ways, the innocent are often involved in the judgment also.

5 But there is always a remnant where grace is found. Noah's family found favor in the eyes of the Lord, so God planned to rescue mankind and start again with the great plan of salvation. This was not to be some easy fix, but raising up a new community of people who would be his family and grow to reestablish his rule on the earth.

6 Not surprisingly, the ark was later taken to refer to the church, the company of believers. This story was a great favorite in the Middle Ages when troupes of mummers (actors) went round from village to village acting out the great stories of the Bible to largely illiterate people. In these plays the ark was God's church, providing an oasis of grace in a wicked world. (Noah's wife in these plays was often a scold and a comic character.)

7 Several simple messages follow from the story. First, we must leave the wicked world and get into the ark. Then, we must help Noah and finally pull others out of the dangerous flood into the ark.

The Story of Abraham: Faith as an Adventure

Genesis 12

The LORD had said to Abram, "Go from your country, your people and your father's household to the land I will show you. I will make you into a great nation, and I will bless you; I will make your name great, and you will be a blessing. I will bless those who bless you, and whoever curses you I will curse; and all peoples on earth will be blessed through you." (vv. 1-3)

See also Hebrews 11:8: *"By faith Abraham, when called to go to a place he would later receive as his inheritance, obeyed and went, even though he did not know where he was going."*

Comment

1 The previous parts of Genesis are a reinterpretation (from God's perspective) of material common to a number of people in the Middle East. However, from chapter 12 on, we are dealing with the Israelites' own family history, the history of God's chosen people, recorded by them in their own tradition. And it begins with God's call and further dealings with their founding father, Abraham, the friend of God.

2 Sin had entered God's creation and spoiled it. However, God did not give up on it but continued working to put it right. Business experts would have set up a commission to find out what was wrong and suggest what to do about it. God went about it a better way. He called a person: Abraham.

3 Abraham was not initially asked to do anything in particular, but simply to get moving. He was not informed as to where he was going, but he was told that God would take care of him, blessing those who were good to him and cursing those who injured him.

4 Abraham was also promised that God would make of him a great nation and that in him and his family, all the people of the earth would be blessed. At this time Abraham was an old man—and childless—yet he trusted God and obeyed. And this is faith: trusting God and setting out on a journey with little or no idea about where we are going. We tend to think of this as a promise and a call to

young people, but it applies also to the old. There is always something, however small, that God wants us to do, and he promises us his help and his blessing too. The Christian life is like this. We put ourselves in God's hands, do what he wants us to do, and then see where it takes us. God also promises to make us a blessing to those around us and even beyond us, and those who mistreat us will not find their life to be easygoing. As the familiar proverb has it, what goes around comes around. Bad people eventually find the going rough.

5 There are many examples of God calling unlikely individuals to achieve his purposes. Dwight L. Moody was a shoe salesman when Christ called him, and he first determined he would be the best shoe salesman he could be. When he noticed a lot of kids in a tough neighborhood who had no connection with any church, he organized a Sunday school class for them. Every Sunday after church he walked around the neighborhood collecting children. Inevitably, someone didn't show up, so he had to teach a class himself. To his surprise he found that he could do it and do it well. One thing led to another, and eventually he became one of the greatest preachers and evangelists of his time. This kind of story could be repeated a million times. If we do what is under our nose, God will open up new avenues of service, and we will discover new abilities and grow more capable as we work. For a start just think of something nice you could do for somebody or say to them. That's not much, but it's a start.

6 This links up with Jesus' parable of the talents (see, e.g., Matt 25). The stewards were given different amounts of money but expected to do what they could with them. The one who was fired had only been given one talent and buried it in the ground. He was blamed, not for doing wrong but for doing nothing. It is not enough to do no harm; we must use the talents God has given us for good, and as we do that, we find that we have other gifts we didn't know we had. We start where we are and see where it takes us.

Jacob's Ladder

Genesis 28; Genesis 32

When he reached a certain place, he stopped for the night because the sun had set. Taking one of the stones there, he put it under his head and lay down to sleep. He had a dream in which he saw a stairway resting on the earth, with its top reaching to heaven, and the angels of God were ascending and descending on it. There above it stood the LORD, and he said: "I

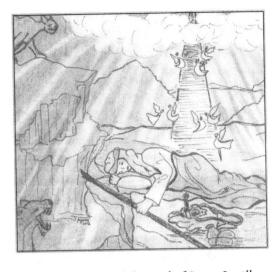

am the LORD, the God of your father Abraham and the God of Isaac. I will give you and your descendants the land on which you are lying." (28:11-13)

That night Jacob got up and took his two wives, his two female servants and his eleven sons and crossed the ford of the Jabbok. After he had sent them across the stream, he sent over all his possessions. So Jacob was left alone, and a man wrestled with him till daybreak. (vv. 22-24)

Read 32:25-31 in your Bible.

Comment

1 This story is about the one selected to be the forefather of the nation of Israel. The Israelites were to be the means of God's plan for the salvation of his world, which had been ruined by sin. One can hardly think of a worse choice. Jacob's name means "supplanter." When Jacob and his twin, Esau, were born, Jacob grabbed his older brother by the heel (Jacob means "one who grasps by the heel," i.e., a tricky wrestler), which describes Jacob perfectly; he was a crafty schemer. He successfully cheated Esau out of his birthright by making him promise to give it up for a good meal when he was starving. With the help of his mother, he later fooled his old blind father, Isaac, into giving him Esau's blessing by covering his

arms with hairy animal skin, making poor old Isaac think that he was blessing hairy Esau. Isaac was a little suspicious, for he said, "The arms are the arms of Esau, but the voice is the voice of Jacob." However, he gave Jacob the blessing due to Esau anyway. It was one thing to get the blessing but another to stay alive long enough to enjoy it. His mother advised him to make a long journey to his uncle Laban in Syria and to stay there until Esau's anger had abated, so he set out. On the first night he had to make a stop in a desolate place with wild animals. He lay down to sleep with a stone for his pillow (to keep his head off the ground) and had a dream where he saw a ladder reaching up to heaven and angels going up and down on it, connecting earth with heaven. The Lord stood above it and repeated the promises he had made to Abraham: to give him and his descendants the land he was lying on, to make of him a great nation, and to bless everyone through him. When he wakened, he said, "Surely the Lord is in this place and I was not aware of it." He used his stony pillow to set up an altar, called the name of the place "Beth-el" (the house of God), and made a vow to the Lord.

2 What did the dream say to Jacob? Clearly it meant that God, who before this was just somebody his father had talked about, was actually real and ruled over heaven and earth.

3 What did he do about this new vision? He made a deal with God. Being Jacob, he bargained hard. If God would keep him safe to reach Uncle Laban in Syria and later bring him home again in peace (not murdered by Esau), then the Lord would be Jacob's God; and of all that he made, he would give God the tithe (one-tenth).

4 Crafty deal or not, God kept his end of the bargain. Jacob reached Uncle Laban's home safely and fell deeply in love with Laban's younger daughter, Rachel. He bargained with Laban to work for him for seven years, at the end of which time he was to receive Rachel as his wife. He worked the seven years, and they seemed as one day for the love he had for her. When the wedding was over, he found that Laban had foisted his older daughter on him, and she had weak eyes, whatever that meant. So they bargained again, for Laban wanted to keep Jacob because things prospered under his hand. The new deal was that Jacob could marry Rachel right away, but in exchange had to work seven more years for Laban. The other terms of the deal were that Jacob could keep all the lambs born that were striped or ringstraked and Laban got the monochromed ones (presumably white). Round three for Laban? Not while playing with crafty Jacob. Jacob devised a scheme for multiplying his share by putting striped and mottled pieces

of tree bark before the eyes of the ewes, which apparently produced striped and ringstraked lambs. Eastern shepherds apparently believe this will work, possibly as a genetic trick to allow lambs to blend in with their surroundings. Uncle Laban changed the terms of the deal seven times with the same result every time, for Jacob simply left in place or removed the strips of bark, and the number of lambs coming to him soared. This was two rogues battling it out, with Jacob—the smarter rogue—coming out ahead every time. Laban could see ruin coming his way, so he finally allowed Jacob to take his wives, children, and flocks and go back home.

5 But Jacob still had to deal with murderous Esau, and he planned well. He camped beside the brook Jabbok and from there sent his servants ahead with generous presents for Esau. They were divided into three bands with a space in between each so that if one was attacked the others could run. Next, he sent his wife Leah and her children with more presents and then dispatched Rachel, his favorite wife. Finally, he kept his most precious possession—himself—safe on the far side of the brook Jabbok.

6 But then a mysterious stranger encountered Jacob and wrestled with him. The struggle went on all night with neither side getting the upper hand. Eventually, the stranger touched the hollow of Jacob's thigh (just over the hip joint), and the joint was wrenched or dislocated (nobody seems to know exactly what happened). Jacob had to give in, but by now he knew who the stranger was, so he grabbed hold of him and would not let go until he got a blessing. He got it, and his name was changed from Jacob to Israel (one who strives with God). Jacob changed the name of the place to Peniel (the face of God), for he had seen God face to face, and his life was preserved.

7 This is a mysterious story and could be interpreted in more than one way (as another deluded dream perhaps engendered by a hard pillow and fear for his life). But there are clear clues sticking out of it, and the last comment in the story is that the sun rose on him as he went on his way. No doubt it did, but there is more to this remark than meets the eye. The sun shone on him in a new way; it was the dawn of a new day for Jacob. He was a different person with a different name and a different character. He still had his faults, but he was no longer the scheming, self-preoccupied Jacob of yore. Rather, he was Israel, a man seeking to do what was good and right. When his sons were about to play a really dirty trick on their pagan neighbors (something the old Jacob might have done), he rebuked them, asking if they wanted their name to stink among the heathen (Gen 34).

8 Several messages emerge from this story:

- That our human nature without God becomes a matter of wanting and getting and is corrupted in the process.

- That God, wanting to change us, encounters us and becomes involved in our life.

- That God even deals kindly with our temporizing and trying to get divine approval cheaply.

- That eventually God confronts us, and we have to deal with him.

- That the result is struggle; it is not easy to give up our own way.

- That as we surrender to our mysterious visitor, a new day dawns, better in every way.

Joseph Overcoming Trouble

Genesis 37

Joseph, the son of Jacob's favorite wife, Rachel, was favored by his father. Jacob gave Joseph a special coat, and his older brothers, born to Leah, were madly jealous. This situation was made even worse when Joseph began to have dreams prophesying that his brothers and even his parents would one day bow down to him. When his brothers were off at a distance looking after the flocks, Joseph was sent out with provisions for them. Their hatred boiled over, and they planned to kill him. But Reuben, one of the more decent brothers, suggested leaving him in a pit instead. Reuben had to go off somewhere, but he was planning to come back and rescue Joseph. Unfortunately, before he returned, the brothers had sold Joseph as a slave to passing Ishmaelite (Arab) traders. Joseph was taken into Egypt and sold to Potiphar, an important Egyptian officer.

Comment

1 Joseph was a young man, just a boy really, when he was taken out of a home where he was loved and cared for and sold into slavery in a foreign land. Whose fault was it? Several people contributed: Jacob's open favoritism certainly did not help. Joseph, too, might have had more sense than to talk openly about his dreams to his already jealous brothers. Mainly, it was his brothers' cruel actions, though. First, they planned to kill him. When his brother Reuben, with some human feeling, suggested an alternative, they dropped Joseph into a pit in the desert with no water, a slow death. Finally, they got rid of him with profit by selling him to some passing merchants. They killed a sheep and dipped his famous coat in it, persuading their father that a wild beast had killed and devoured him.

2 Joseph became a slave in the house of Potiphar, down at the very bottom of the social heap. Joseph could indeed have felt angry not only with his brothers but even with the God he had heard about in his home, who had allowed this to happen. But I think that he was sustained by his faith, wisely discussed the matter with God, and was no doubt assured that God was in charge and that good would come out of it somehow, sometime. So his faith sustained him, and he did the best he could in the situation and soon obtained a position of trust in Potiphar's household.

3 But worse was yet to come. Joseph was a handsome lad, and Potiphar's naughty wife propositioned him when Potiphar was away on business, and indeed sought to take him by force. But Joseph was appalled at the idea of such immorality and disloyalty to his master, so he ran out of the house. Potiphar's wife held on to Joseph's cloak and used it as evidence for her claim that Joseph had attempted to rape her. Joseph was put in prison. Despite his good response to hard fate, here he was back at the bottom of the heap again.

4 Joseph held on to his firm faith in God and again did his best in the bad situation. Indeed, he even rose to a position of trust in the prison. He did not whine about his own fate but tried to be helpful to his fellow prisoners. Two of these prisoners had dreams. Pharaoh's chief butler dreamed about a vine with three branches loaded with ripe grapes, which he pressed into juice and gave to Pharaoh. Joseph told him that the three branches were three days and that on the third day he would be restored to Pharaoh's favor—which he was. The chief baker dreamed that he had three baskets of bread on his head and the birds of the air came and devoured the contents of the top basket. Joseph told him that on the third day he would be taken out and executed. Joseph was here again doing what good he could to those around him. But we would be wrong if we thought Joseph was happy about his situation. He had done nothing wrong; in fact, it was quite the reverse. He asked the official who was going to be restored to Pharaoh's favor to remember him and get him out of there. He still had hard feelings about his brothers for what they had done to him, and he eventually expressed these feelings and dealt with them.

5 This, then, is a story of undeserved disaster, which could be found often enough even in our own relatively ordinary circumstances, where people or circumstances are hostile to us without any misdoing on our part. They may try to hurt or hinder us, perhaps with success. In the great world outside, Christians are seriously oppressed and even persecuted. Many of them respond with wonderful courage and faith, just as Joseph did, trying to do what good they can. Think of Stephen's martyrdom and the way he prayed for his murderers (see Acts 7).

6 We have been considering here how Joseph dealt with disaster. In our next rest stop we will be studying how he dealt with the even greater test of character: success.

A Change of Fortune for Joseph

Genesis 40–42

While he was in prison, Joseph had interpreted the dream of Pharaoh's cup-bearer, telling him he would be restored to his office and asking the butler to remember him when that happened. Of course, the cupbearer forgot all about it until, two years later, Pharaoh had a couple dreams that none of his wise men could interpret (the seven thin cattle devouring the seven fat ones, etc.). Then the cupbearer remembered Joseph, and he was brought to the palace to interpret the dreams. They foretold, Joseph said, seven good years followed by seven years of famine. Pharaoh was so impressed by Joseph's wisdom and manner that he put him in charge of the preparations for the famine. In fact, he gave Joseph his ring of office and made him the viceroy of all Egypt.

Joseph built great storehouses and filled them with food that he was able to purchase at a bargain price in the years of plenty. When the famine years came, Joseph had food to sell to those in need. When Jacob heard there was corn in Egypt, he sent all his older sons there to buy food. But he kept Benjamin, the youngest, Rachel's second child, at home with him.

When the brothers reached Egypt, Joseph recognized them, although they did not know him in all his glory. Yet he did not make himself known to them right away. He must have had some lingering resentment left in him, for he tormented them quite a bit. He accused them of being spies and forced them to bring Benjamin down to see him, ostensibly to show that they had been telling him the truth. He then hid his silver cup in Benjamin's sack, which made Benjamin liable to enslavement, if not the death penalty, for stealing the viceroy's valuable cup. In their terror the brothers concluded that this awful fate was the result of the wrong that they had done to Joseph. To give them credit, they made all sorts of unselfish proposals to save Benjamin from being enslaved in Egypt. But at this point Joseph could not carry out his revenge any further. He had to slip away so they would not see him weeping. When he returned, he disclosed himself to his brothers and embraced them with tears. They were shattered and probably terrified, expecting the worst, but Joseph told them not to blame themselves, for it was all part of God's plan to rescue and provide for the family of promise. Pharaoh heard about Joseph's father and brought the entire family to Egypt and settled them in the land of Goshen.

Comment

1 Does this story insinuate that God deliberately put it into the hearts of the brothers to wickedly mistreat and sell Joseph so that he might end up viceroy of Egypt and preserve their family, which had a special place in God's plans? Hardly. Rather, it is that God weaves bad things into his plan to achieve good. This is a big theme in the Bible and a great comfort to us when we fail, make bad decisions, and take wrong turns. The old master carpet makers in the East sat behind the carpet and called the shots while the whole family, including the children, did the actual work on the front side. If one of the children put in a few wrong stitches, it was a point of honor for the master weaver never to have the wrong stitches removed but rather to redesign the pattern to include the mistakes. So it is with God and our mistakes. In marvelous ways he turns them to good.

A Stroll Through the Bible

2 What do you think about the cruel tricks Joseph played on his brothers? Did he have to torment them to make them realize the extent of their evil? What do you think he should have done?

3 Even if we conclude that a better course would have been to reveal himself to his brothers right away, he drew up short in his revenge and wept and embraced them. It is a good thing, when we are overwhelmed with anger at wrongs done to us or even to others, to stop short and regroup, considering how much God has forgiven us. The wrath of man worketh not the righteousness of God (Jas 1:20).

4 Perhaps the most important point to note in this wonderful story is that success and prosperity did not spoil or corrupt Joseph. People who have struggled up from the bottom of the heap to prosperity can become confused as to the direction they should take next. If they cannot get a good answer to this question, their lives can take a turn for the worse. They can go on to pile up wealth upon wealth or honor upon honor when they should rather consider what good they can do with what has been given to them. Sam Walton started a small business that eventually blossomed into a massive chain of stores. When he was asked what he most liked about his success, he said it gave him pleasure to go into a store and see people with a job. If we do not feel that we are doing good in what we are doing, we will not enjoy what we do, nor will we do it well.

5 A young lawyer, speaking to our Christian law students at Campbell University, told how he was in a hotel near the World Trade Center in New York City during the terrorist attack there. He was frightened out of his wits and knelt down and promised God that if he got out of this alive, things would be different; he would live for God. What do you think happened when he arrived home and went to the office? Back to business as usual? He was surprised to find on Monday that his whole attitude toward work, toward people, and toward life in general had been turned inside out. His clients were now people. His skills and abilities were now aimed at doing good, and success was no longer just about making money and being acclaimed as an up-and-coming lawyer. He also became involved in all sorts of charitable work in third-world countries. Do you think he now enjoys his work more than he used to? His former life was phony; his current life is real. It is eternal life being lived now.

The Birth and Rescue of Baby Moses

Exodus 2

There was a man from the family of Levi who decided to marry a woman from the tribe of Levi. She became pregnant and gave birth to a baby boy. The mother saw how beautiful the baby was and hid him for three months, after which time she made a basket and covered it with tar so it would float. Then she put the baby in the basket and put the basket in the river in the tall grass. The baby's sister stayed and kept watch to make sure the baby was okay. When Pharaoh's daughter went to the river to bathe, she heard the baby crying and found the basket. She felt sorry for the crying baby. Then she noticed he was one of the Hebrew babies. The baby's sister was still hiding. She stood up and asked the king's daughter, "Do you want me to go find a Hebrew woman who can nurse the baby and help you care for it?" The king's daughter replied, "Yes, please." So the girl went and brought the baby's own mother. The king's daughter said to the mother, "Take this baby and feed him for me. I'll pay you to take care of him." So the woman took her baby and cared for him. The baby grew, and after some time the woman gave the baby to the king's daughter, who accepted the baby as her own son. She named him Moses because she had pulled him from the water.

Comment

1 As the giver of the Law and the leader of the exodus from Egypt, Moses was, perhaps along with Abraham, the leader and founder of the race, the most important person in Israel. To speak against Moses was to be worthy of death. God's hand was upon him from the beginning. He was saved from the death sentence pronounced by Pharaoh on all Hebrew boys when his mother hid him in the bushes beside the Nile. Pharaoh's daughter found and adopted him, and he was given the Egyptian name *Moses*, which means "rescued from the water."

2 Moses was educated and brought up in Pharaoh's palace, trained in hunting and manly sports and exercises appropriate to a prince. Perhaps more importantly, he would be prepared to exercise authority, to take charge and get things done. All this prepared him for the great work God had in mind for him: to rescue the Israelites from slavery, lead them to the promised land, and generally prepare them to be the family and people of God.

3 We are not Moses, and our circumstances are quite different from his, but the message is the same: God has things for us to do. They may be large or small, but they are all important; and throughout our early life he has been preparing us for them.

4 How do we know what is God's plan for our life? We don't, but if we do well what he has set before us today, tomorrow's task will appear and our gifts and talents will expand to meet it. The old childhood chorus has it right:

> Trust and obey
> For there's no other way
> To be happy in Jesus
> But to trust and obey.

The Call of Moses:
Servant of God

Exodus 1–2

Joseph's family had settled in Egypt, which had become quite a nation. But a new Pharaoh arose who "knew not Joseph," and he enslaved the Israelites. As they became numerous, he became afraid of a slave revolt and ordered the midwives to start drowning any Hebrew baby boys. Moses's parents were able to hide him until he was three months old, but then they put him in a waterproof basket and hid him in the reeds bordering the Nile, with his older sister Miriam to keep watch.

When Pharaoh's daughter came with her maidens for her morning bath in the Nile, she heard the child crying, found him, and adopted him as her son. Though he was in Pharaoh's palace, he knew he was a Hebrew, not an Egyptian. He became curious and went to have a look at his people. When he found an Egyptian overseer beating a Hebrew slave, his anger flared up, and he killed he Egyptian and buried the body in the sand. The next day he saw two Hebrews fighting and rebuked them. One of them said, "Will you kill me like you did the Egyptian?" Moses knew Pharaoh would soon hear about his deed, so he took off into the desert to avoid being arrested and executed.

Eventually, Moses settled down in the mountain region of Midian with Jethro, a Midianite priest. He married a couple of Jethro's daughters and had sons by them and looked after his father-in-law's sheep. But then God called him. Moses saw a bush burning, a common enough sight in the desert, but this bush kept burning and seemed none the worse for it. Moses turned aside to see this strange sight. God then called out of the fire, "Moses, Moses," and Moses replied, "Here I am." God said, "Take off your sandals, for you are on holy ground." God then told Moses that he had heard the cry of the oppressed Hebrews and was sending Moses to them with the good news. Moses was no doubt pleased with the good news but far from pleased that he had to play a leading part in this deliverance. He raised all sorts of objections, but God countered all his misgivings and promised to be with him. In the end he had to go.

Comment

1 Moses wanted to know God's name since the Hebrews would ask him who had sent him. God answered, "My name is EHWH" ("I Am" in Hebrew). So when Moses was asked who sent him, he said, "JHWH" ("He is"). This was translated by Moffat as "the Eternal" since God always was and always will be. This name of God was too sacred to be bandied about, and the Jews are thought to have used ADONAI ("the Lord") as a substitute. In Hebrew writing there are only a few written vowels so that the spoken vowels had to be added by the Masoretic editors. They did this with little marks around the letters called pointing. It has been surmised that the vowels of ADONAI (points) were added to the consonants JHWH, and much later it was assumed that the name of God was JEHOVAH.

2 The second commandment forbids us to take the name of God on our lips lightly. Our forefathers took this seriously and only used the name of God reverently, as in prayer when we say "Our Father." An Irish Methodist minister, Reverend Jim Rea, was writing recently to a Belfast newspaper about this and noted how easily the name of God or of Christ has become part of ordinary conversation. This is bound to be offensive to those who reverence God. Should we reprove them? At any rate we should not tacitly agree with them but by our expression and attitude let it be known how we feel. In the end they may appreciate the inappropriateness of using the name of God lightly or even worse, cursing. I remember once in my wild youth when I was showing off with a mouthful of bad language. A young girl told me I shouldn't talk that way. It shut my mouth, for I knew she was right, and I thought highly of her and appreciated her polite rebuke.

3 Moses was given a number of proofs to authenticate his claim to speak for God. We do not have such obvious credentials. But do we need them? Jesus has promised to be with us as God was with Moses, and we ourselves by our manner of living are to be our own authentication—living letters of credit as St. Paul put it (2 Cor 3:2).

4 The Bible is not ready to produce miracles for all occasions. In fact, they only appear at important points in the divine history. Their purpose is not to provide a firework display but to teach us important lessons about what is going on (they are described as signs). Miracles thus appeared at the liberation of the Hebrews to be God's special people. Then they disappear until the coming of the prophets. There are no more until Jesus' birth and later when the teaching function of his miracles is prominent and obvious. Jesus' ministry was the coming of

the kingdom of God, and the miracles describe this plainly (the lame walk, the blind see, and the kingdom of God is preached to the poor). The next group of miracles occur to explain Jesus' sacrifice on the cross (the darkness over the land and the veil of the temple torn in two, opening up the holy presence of God to all believers). Then there are the miracles surrounding the resurrection, and finally the great miracle of the day of Pentecost when the hearers heard the apostles' words each in their own native language, presaging the preaching of the gospel to all nations. Later miracles, especially healings, accompanied the preaching of the good news to the Jews and later to the Gentiles by Paul and his companions.

5 Moses was a prophet, one who was sent by God to speak in God's name. Some folks in the camp started to do the same, but Moses's sidekicks stopped them. Moses rebuked his supporters, saying, "Would God that all the Lord's people were prophets." We may not be as powerful as Moses, but we are all sent by God to speak and act in his name.

6 Like Moses, we generally feel inadequate and want to back out. "There must be somebody better qualified than I am," we think. That is probably true, but God delights in calling the less obviously talented (like the first disciples called and appointed by Jesus).

Moses Convincing Pharaoh

Exodus 5–11

God told Moses and Aaron to go and tell Pharaoh to let the Hebrews go on a three-day journey into the desert to sacrifice to their God. The departure into the desert was, Moses said, because the religious rites of the Hebrews would be offensive to the Egyptians. Pharaoh was contemptuous ("Who is this God that I should obey him?") and refused. Ten plagues followed his refusal.

Comment

1 The ten plagues of Egypt at first sight seem incredible, so one might easily conclude that the Israelites made them up. This is very unlikely. It is perhaps easier to believe that these were real events that they, or Moses, interpreted as miracles. It has been suggested that the first miracle, the waters turning to blood, was really a toxic bacterial bloom, which can be red. This would drive the frogs out of the water, where they would eventually die and rot, providing an excellent medium for a plague of flies to develop. The stings of these flies would lead to skin problems and even boils. Even the final plague, the death of the firstborn of both Egyptians and their animals, which is a really tough one to explain, is allegedly due to the custom of allowing the firstborn male to eat first. Since the food would come from the topmost layer of the storage container, the one most likely to become contaminated during storage, the firstborn male would get the fatal dose. This is a harder explanation to swallow, for it does not tell us why the firstborn animals also died. Did they get first crack at the fodder?

2 It is probably better to see this series of events, as Moses saw it, as the mighty hand of God intervening to allow his people to go free and begin their long preparation for the role God had assigned to them and their descendants. Even if some natural series of events produced the results, they happened under the hand of the Almighty, who controls all nature and can press the buttons and pull the switches as and when he wishes. But who knows? Moses was there, and we were not.

3 But the exodus was a mighty event, one requiring signs to interpret it. These miracles and those that followed later demonstrated that JHWH, the God of Israel, was in complete charge and was about to set up his new plan of salvation by taking this helpless band of slaves out of Egypt to the promised land. Thus, he would fulfill his promise to Abraham that in him and his seed, all the families of the earth would be blessed. The gods of the Egyptians, which they had become accustomed to during the long years in Egypt, were nothing.

The Crossing of the Red Sea

Exodus 14

The children of Israel were eventually allowed to leave Egypt and set out into the desert. Their Egyptian neighbors provided them with all that they needed (they pillaged the Egyptians). They were proceeding round the north end of the Gulf of Suez, which flows into the Red Sea (the shortest route to Palestine), but God redirected them to detour south, enter a narrow valley at Migdol leading to the shore of the Gulf of Suez, and camp there. But Pharaoh had changed his mind again and pursued them with his chariots

(the panzer tank corps of the day), so the Israelites were trapped between the sea in front and the Egyptian army behind. They began, as usual, to complain to Moses ("Were there no graves in Egypt that you had to bring us out here to be killed?"). But Moses said to them, "Stand still, and see what the Lord will do." God commanded him to stretch forth his staff, and the waters divided so that the Israelites crossed over on dry ground during the night. When the Egyptians tried to follow them in the morning, the waters returned, and they were all drowned.

Comment

1 This story is not as ridiculous as it sounds. The Gulf of Suez, leading to the Red Sea, is mile-deep elsewhere, but at Migdol, between the two narrow valleys on either side, silt from the rivers had piled up, producing a causeway only a few hundred feet below the surface. Exodus 14 provides some details of the event. A cold wind blew all that night through the valleys and piled up the waters on either side of the causeway. This effect can be demonstrated using an electric fan. The cold and powerful wind could then freeze the waters in position so the Israelites crossed over on dry ground. But when the Egyptians tried to follow them in the

morning, the sun would have risen and melted the ice walls so that the waters crashed back into position and swept them away; not one of them survived. Divers have reported and photographed chariot wheels half-buried in the sand at the crossing point (skeptics will claim the photographs may be forged and want one of the wheels brought up for carbon dating). I am not saying that this is exactly what happened, only that it could have happened this way and that the detailed description of the events in Exodus fits into this picture rather well. Yet it is not to be thought that the event, explained in this way, is less miraculous. Miracles are only mysterious to us. God is in charge of all of nature, and he presses the buttons and throws the switches to work his will.

2 This miraculous event, right at the beginning of the history of the Hebrews, has been commemorated ever since in the Seder, the Passover ritual meal. And this great miracle was indeed a sign designed to show the Israelites that their God, JHWH, was the Lord of all nature and that all other so-called gods, such as the gods of the Egyptians, were mere idols created by human hands, with no power to save. The first of the Ten Commandments expresses this: I am the Lord who brought you out of the land of Egypt, out of the house of bondage; you shall have no other gods besides me.

3 We will see later in the Israelites' story that when they settled in the promised land, they were tempted to copy their pagan neighbors, who were more experienced farmers, and bow down and worship gods of stone and wood and precious metal. We, in our age and circumstances, are not so tempted, but there are other gods besides the ancient images. We can worship at the shrine of political powers, even religious ones, and also cultures and philosophies. Even science, one of God's greatest and most divine gifts to us, can be, and has been, an idol raised up to dazzle us and entice us away from our higher allegiance. Many of these idols, like the Nazi and Communist empires, are downright evil and need to be resisted in the name of the living and true God.

4 These false gods cannot save, and one by one they collapse in a cloud of dust. Shelley's famous poem "Ozymandias" expresses the futility of all human idols. The enormous statue of himself built by Pharaoh Ramses II lay shattered and buried in the sand. Nobody remembers who Ozimandias was or what he did.

5 We need to remember the even mightier acts of God—in creation, in the coming of his son Jesus Christ, in the resurrection, in the establishment of the church (the new Israel)—and bow down to him and serve him alone. His kingdom is forever and ever. All others are fleeting and transient.

The Ten Commandments, Part 1

Exodus 20

And God spoke all these words:

"I am the LORD your God, who brought you out of Egypt, out of the land of slavery.

"You shall have no other gods before me.

"You shall not make for yourself an image in the form of anything in heaven above or on the earth beneath or in the waters below. You shall not bow down to them or worship them; for I, the LORD your God, am a jealous God, punishing the children for the sin of the parents to the third and fourth generation of those who hate me, but showing love to a thousand generations of those who love me and keep my commandments.

"You shall not misuse the name of the LORD your God, for the LORD will not hold anyone guiltless who misuses his name.

"Remember the Sabbath day by keeping it holy." (vv. 1-8)

Comment

1 The Law of Moses divides conveniently into two parts. The second and much longer part considers all sorts of legal disputes and provides rulings for them. These materials are similar (though with significant changes) to those found in the other Middle East codes, such as the Code of Hammurabi and the Egyptian code. The earlier and much smaller part is the Decalogue, the Ten Commandments. None of the other Middle Eastern codes have anything like this. These commandments are the basic principles that govern the detailed rules that follow. The first four concern our relationship with God, and the first of these is the foundation of all the rest. He is the Lord and must be first in everything. God comes first, and we must be careful to keep God as king and ruler of our lives.

2 The second commandment forbids the worship of graven images. God cannot be represented by any earthly images. Bad practices, such as sacrificing children, were commonly associated with them, so they were forbidden. The Israelites were surrounded by superstitious neighbors who believed that worshiping such things brought them luck. They were also experienced farmers, so the Israelites,

who were beginners in agriculture, would be tempted to follow their example. Finally, the Israelites intermarried with the sons and daughters of their Canaanite neighbors, who would bring their idols and their practices with them into the home. How does all of this relate to us? Could we too have a bad or inadequate image of God (too soft or too harsh; too distant and unreal), and might this affect our lives? Can we put people or things in the place intended for God alone, at the center of our lives and homes: things like our children, our careers, our material possessions, or our reputation? Have we, inadvertently perhaps, absorbed notions from our surrounding people that are diluting and warping our Christian ideals and standards?

3 The third commandment has to do with taking the name of the Lord thoughtlessly and irreverently on our lips. If we love and reverence God, we should have a conscience about taking the name of God or of Christ too lightly on our lips. And when people around us sound off like this, it should be offensive to us, and they should know it, by our attitude and practice, even without our saying anything to them about it. We would be annoyed if someone used the name of a loved one, say your mother, casually like this, and it should be the same with the name of God. People can quickly sense your feeling that this is offensive without your saying anything, and you can explain your feelings, if asked, in terms of their respect for their close family members.

4 The fourth commandment concerns a day of rest and worship, like the Jewish Sabbath. This was originally held on the last day of the week (Saturday). But early Christians transferred it to the first day (Sunday) as the day of the resurrection. It does not really matter which day we keep differently, though it is good if we share the same day as much as possible. It is also important that we rest and recuperate from the stresses of the week to avoid burnout. It is also intended to be a day of spiritual refreshment; substituting the beach or golf for church is a bad choice (at least go to church at the beach). And it is a great time to read the Bible, for pleasure as much as for profit. There are lots of helpful books that might be taken up on Sunday. A businessman with a terminal disease got talking to his minister and complained that he never had time to read the Bible. His minister, Reverend Leslie Weatherhead, hardly a conservative, thought to himself that he was seventy years old. How many Sundays did that add up to?

5 We also need to remember how Jesus healed on the Sabbath to the horror of the orthodox Jews. It is a day to do good: visit somebody sick or distressed, write a letter to somebody, etc.

The Ten Commandments, Part 2

Exodus 20

"Honor your father and your mother, so that you may live long in the land the LORD your God is giving you.

"You shall not murder.

"You shall not commit adultery.

"You shall not steal.

"You shall not give false testimony against your neighbor.

"You shall not covet your neighbor's house. You shall not covet your neighbor's wife, or his male or female servant, his ox or donkey, or anything that belongs to your neighbor". (vv. 12-17)

Comment

1 The last six commandments concern daily living. All are general principles that guide the application of particular rules; they are not themselves such rules.

2 The fifth has to do with the family. Without a stable family there can be no health in the nation, and if any society forgets or loses this, its days will not be long. It will become chaotic and weak. Delinquency and other evils will surely follow. We have seen this in our own time.

3 The sixth relates to the sacredness of human life. To take away the life of someone, even if they are guilty of horrible crimes, is a serious matter. You will gather at this point that I am not in favor of the death penalty. There are two reasons for this. First, the criminal justice system is far from perfect, and wrongful convictions for serious crimes are by no means rare. Second, it prevents offenders from repenting and becoming good people, which also is not unknown, especially with young offenders. It will also be obvious that I am uneasy about abortion. A child is a little miracle, a gift from the hand of God, and should be treated as such. What I am really opposing, without any exceptions, are social abortions, unfortunately the vast majority nowadays. To kill a baby for the parent's convenience, or to prevent social embarrassment, is to my mind inexcusable. It is bad for the mother, who often ends up with serious guilt problems. There is also no good social argument for it since there are good people eager to adopt babies.

In my medical practice I strongly urged single young women to avoid abortion and elect to deliver their babies. Almost all were happy to do so. On the very rare occasion I could sense I was wasting my breath, I gave them the telephone number of a reputable clinic where at least the procedure would be carried out in sterile circumstances. My happiest experience in medical practice was when a young teenage girl had become involved with a married man who had no intention of marrying her. When the pregnancy test showed positive, she begged me not to tell her father. I had to tell him, and he supported her loyally. When she came to the hospital for delivery, there was a nice young man with her who wished to help raise the baby as his own. I delivered the baby and married them the next day. If that happened every day, I would still be in medical practice.

4 The seventh commandment deals with adultery, defined as having sexual relations with another man's wife or with a woman's husband. It is not a general principle dealing with sexual morals (that was covered in later detailed rules); it concerns the sanctity of the marriage relationship. So seriously was this taken that both parties were stoned to death. But divorce was allowed, provided the wife was returned to her family along with her marriage portion.

5 The eighth commandment forbids stealing. This is spelled out in some detail in the later regulations, but the basic principle is honesty, a mighty virtue to be practiced by every Christian as a major component of their testimony. For as Robbie Burns has so aptly put it, "An honest man though aye so puir is king of men for a' that."

6 The ninth commandment only deals with false testimony in legal proceedings, for abuse of legal proceedings was common and often involved false witnesses (see the story of Naboth's vineyard in 1 Kgs 21). But again, the underlying principle is honesty so that your word can be relied on. This is another mighty virtue that commends us in the sight of all men. Aquinas would tell us that there are exceptions to every rule, so it can be proper and even necessary to lie (or, for that matter, to kill). But even though it is right in such circumstances, one immediately loses one's reputation for honesty and perhaps one's self-respect. Breaking the ninth commandment, even when justified, comes at a price.

7 The final commandment is the only one relating to motive rather than action. It forbids coveting anything that belongs to your neighbor. How one could enforce this as a positive rule of law is not easy to see, but the great principle of neighborliness is involved. This command is fulfilled in the golden rule of the New Testament that we are to love our neighbor as ourselves.

A Stroll Through the Bible

The Blessed and the Accursed Life

Deuteronomy 27:11-26

On the same day Moses commanded the people:

When you have crossed the Jordan, these tribes shall stand on Mount Gerizim to bless the people: Simeon, Levi, Judah, Issachar, Joseph and Benjamin. And these tribes shall stand on Mount Ebal to pronounce curses: Reuben,

Gad, Asher, Zebulun, Dan and Naphtali.

The Levites shall recite to all the people of Israel in a loud voice:

"Cursed is anyone who makes an idol—a thing detestable to the LORD, the work of skilled hands—and sets it up in secret."

Then all the people shall say, "Amen!" (vv. 11-15)

Read through verse 26 in your Bible.

Comment

1 In the Bible the notions of loving (*ahav* is to love) and hating (*sane* is to hate) and blessing (*baraq*) and cursing (*ra'ah*) are not quite what we would understand by those words today. It is said of Jacob and Esau, "Jacob I loved, but Esau I hated" (Rom 9:13), but Esau was loved and protected by God. It is simply that the promise given to Abraham and his seed was to be fulfilled through the younger brother Jacob's descendants, not Esau's. Perhaps "preferred" and "rejected" would be better renderings of love and hate here. Similarly, blessing and cursing are a little different in the Bible. For us to put a curse on anyone is to wish all kinds of bad things to happen to them. In the Bible to be accursed means that if you are walking outside the right way, bad things will happen to you. "The way of the transgressor is hard" (Prov 13:15), so God's promise to Abraham that he would bless those who blessed him and curse those who cursed him was a statement of

the facts of our living conditions, not about malice and hatred as we understand them.

2 In the Beatitudes Jesus was stating as a matter of fact that the meek who did not live for themselves, but for others, would be blessed. In fact, when all the strong were gone and forgotten, the work of the unselfish would still be there producing a harvest of good things. Napoleon's mighty works are dust; John Wesley's are still going strong. For the works, great or small, of all good people last.

3 Consider all the bad things the accursed were doing in Moses's day. What are such people doing today? What will be the end result of all their struggles and doings? Not much. But of the children of God it is said, "Blessed are the dead who die in the Lord from now on.... They will rest from their labor, for their deeds will follow them" (Rev 14:13). In other words, the good results of their work will keep going.

4 We see this principle of God blessing our works in the lives of the great servants of God, but it also applies in the lives and works of us ordinary people. Everything we do for God and for those around us is like good seed planted in the ground. God will bring unexpected good things out of it, which will continue unfolding into the future. Consider also Jesus' parable of the good seed (Matt 13), which produces good crops: some thirty, some sixty, and some a hundredfold.

5 Moses told the people, "This day I call the heavens and the earth as witnesses against you that I have set before you life and death, blessings and curses. Now choose life, so that you and your children may live" (Deut 30:19), and his words still hold for us today. The things we do or say for God and for our neighbors, however small and apparently insignificant they may appear to us, are alive and continuing to do good under God's blessing. But the rest, even when they seem to promise greatness, are just chaff, blown away by the winds of time.

6 This scene was more or less repeated when Joshua, who had taken over from Moses, gathered the tribes of Israel toward the end of his career and reminded them of all that the Lord had done for them. He went on to challenge them that if it seemed evil for them to serve the Lord to choose whom they would serve. Notice that he did not ask them to choose *if* they would serve. We will inevitably serve either God or some pretended deity, and the choice will again be either life or death, blessing or cursing; there is nothing in between. By electing not to choose God, we do not have the option of freedom. It is either serve God or serve a worse, much worse, master (see Josh 24:15).

Manna from Heaven

Exodus 15:23-26

As the Israelites continued their journey through the desert, they inevitably encountered water and food shortages. In the first of these, the water was bitter and undrinkable. As usual, they complained to Moses. But God instructed Moses to cast a certain tree into the water, and it became sweet. Then they were starving and ready to stone Moses and Aaron. But God sent flocks of birds every evening for meat and in the morning a strange substance for bread. It was described as being like coriander seed and tasted sweet like honey. They did not know what it was, so they called it "manna" (meaning "What is it?"). They had to gather it every morning, for it did not keep until the next day, except on the eve of the Sabbath when they could collect two days' supply. Another crisis—this time a water shortage—was met when Moses was commanded by God to strike a rock and sweet water flowed out of it.

Comment

1 In Hebrew *manna* translates "What is it?" for that is what the Israelites said when they saw it. Many explanations of the heavenly bread exist, some more plausible than others, but the message is clearly about God supplying our needs when all else fails. We do not expect God to feed and supply us in good times, but people who are responsible for the helpless often have to ask God for supplies. The famous Dr. Muller, who ran an orphanage in Bristol, England, was often desperate to provide food for his charges. On one morning when the cupboard was bare, a bread van rolled up to the door, left a full complement of loaves, and drove off. A rather odd example was when Dr. James Archibald Campbell, the founder of what would become Campbell University in North Carolina, was constructing a building with many willing hands but no money. The work was going very slowly because they were sawing logs by hand and needed a sawmill. They became discouraged and decided to go fishing. Believe it or not, a sawmill came floating down the river. Dr. Campbell, a great believer in the power of prayer, was loudly praising the Lord when one of his helpers noticed the name of an upriver lumber company stamped on it. Dr Campbell was persuaded to phone the owner,

who gladly gave the sawmill to the budding school. Coincidence? You would be wasting your time trying to persuade Dr. Campbell of that.

2 The birds supplying meat is not too difficult to understand as large flocks of migrating birds get tired at the end of the day and are easy to catch, but attempts to explain the manna in ordinary terms have not been persuasive. So God's provision for the Israelites is like his care for us: you believe it or you don't. But Moses placed a jar of manna in the ark of the covenant (and apparently it didn't rot). The ark was later moved from place to place to preserve it in dangerous times, and it is allegedly still surviving in Ethiopia with a keeper appointed for life to watch over it. Nobody else is allowed to see the ark or examine its contents. Wouldn't we like to take a peek into it and see if the Ten Commandments and the jar of manna were still there? But these items are so priceless that somebody would plan to steal them. The Nazis were eager to get possession of such things.

3 Jesus told us not to be anxious about our daily needs (Matt 6:31), and St. Paul advises us not to be anxious about anything, but in everything by prayer and supplication make our requests known to God, for "my God will meet all your needs" (Phil 4:19).

4 God has to work in the background. The kingdom of heaven is like seed sown in the ground; the crop grows quietly and unobserved (Mark 4). So it is with prayer. John Wesley used to encourage his class meetings to make a note of all the things they prayed for. They were surprised to find how many had been answered over time. We found the same thing in one of our weekly prayer meetings in our law school. God moves so quietly that we often do not notice what he is doing.

5 We are also told to keep praying. Jesus told a story of a hard-hearted judge who didn't fear God and cared nothing for anybody else, yet he granted a poor widow's request because she wore him down with her persistence (Luke 18). This is not to say God is like the judge, rather that we must pray with persistence.

6 Above all we are told not to be anxious about the necessities of life. Even the sparrows are fed, and we are of much more value than them (Matt 10).

Samson:
A Strong Man with Serious Weaknesses

Judges 13–16

There was a man called Manoah whose wife was barren. An angel visited her and told her she would bear a special child and that she was not to drink wine or take any unclean food. Her son was to be a "Nazarite," and in addition to avoiding wine and unclean food, his hair was never to be cut or he would forfeit his great strength.

He was indeed a mighty man, and with only the jawbone of an ass, he killed a great number of the enemy. He also tied foxes together with flaming torches on their tails and set them loose in the corn fields of the enemy.

He judged Israel for about twenty years, and we hear much of his might but little of his wisdom. He became enamored by a Philistine woman, Delilah, and insisted on marrying her, but she betrayed him over and over again to the Philistine lords for money, ever seeking to discover for them the secret of his strength. Samson fooled her several times but eventually told her the real source of his strength. She had the seven locks of his hair cut off while he was asleep on her knees. The Philistine lords were then able to take and bind him and carry him off as a prisoner to Gath, one of their cities, where they blinded him and otherwise made sport with him.

Eventually, his hair began to grow back, and he prayed to God that he might be given back his strength just one more time. He was brought into the temple of Dagon, the god of the Philistines, on a feast day, but before the sport began, he seized the two pillars of the temple and with one mighty heave pulled the building down so that he killed more enemies in his death than he had in his life.

Comment

1 This is a sad story of a man who was given extraordinary gifts to save his people but whose character flaws got in the way, leading to his ignominious end. This story could be repeated many times with talented Christian leaders with similar flaws.

2 Young ministers are commonly advised by their elders to choose their life partners wisely, and for the most part I believe they do. The careers of many ministers with limited abilities have been greatly enhanced by gifted wives. Our lady ministers, too, often have cause to bless their spouses who work along with them. Two heads and hearts are better than one.

3 There are also bad career choices, generally motivated by financial prospects and even a desire to be considered successful and admired. Our portrayal to our children of what we consider a good choice of career is often flawed. We should consider what career will contribute most to mankind in general and fit in with what God may be planning for our lives. I can think of two important careers that are often downplayed, namely becoming ministers of the gospel and elementary school teachers. Their importance is not to be measured by financial rewards or even public applause but by more important considerations.

4 Even when we have made a choice of a particular career, the way in which we carry out our duties and conduct our business can be flawed, and here one's faith makes a difference. Carrying out our duties from the wrong motives can be just as destructive as failing to do them. When Christ comes into our lives, he wants to get into our work. When he does, we begin to see things differently. We are no longer working for material gain, praise, or reputation. We see people differently too, as Jesus saw them, and we are sustained in the trials of work by the conviction that we are doing good and so doing God's will. This principle holds in any profession or occupation. In early days we are concerned with making a living and becoming competent and safe, but after a few years that is not enough. We need a better motive driving our work. If we do not get it, we will not enjoy it much and probably will not do it very well.

5 This sad story has a more hopeful end. Samson, blinded and humiliated, turned once more to God and asked for the strength for one more effort. And he got it. Many of us look back on our lives with thankfulness but also sometimes with sadness, to think on things not attempted and time wasted on lesser things. But it is never too late to ask for the strength for one more effort, even if it seems small to us—an encouraging word or a kind deed that God can bless and bring good out of. We can always finish well.

God Can Work with Few as Well as Many

Judges 7

The book of Judges tells how, again and again, the Israelites forsook their God who had brought them out of the land of Egypt into the promised land, adopting the religion and practices of their heathen neighbors, erecting altars to Baal, and planting sacred groves of trees for their religious rites. Every time they did this, they became weak and were oppressed by surrounding powers, one after another. They cried unto God in their misery, and he heard them and sent them deliverers (judges) who rescued them. And at least while the judge lived, they returned to the God of their fathers. But when the judge died, they relapsed again (or at least the succeeding generation did), and the story repeated itself.

One of the more interesting stories of the book of Judges concerns Gideon at the time when the Midianites were coming like a swarm of locusts every harvest time, devouring all the food and leaving the Israelites to starve. Gideon was hiding in a winepress threshing some wheat when an angel appeared to him and told him he was chosen to deliver Israel and that God would be with him. He offered the usual excuses, as Moses had done before him, and demanded signs to assure him that God was really with him. He took a fleece and laid it on the ground. When the morning dew arrived, the fleece was dry, and the threshing floor was wet. That was not enough for him, so he repeated the test with the fleece becoming wet and the ground remaining dry. Convinced at last, he went out and threw down the family altar of Baal and cut down the sacred grove.

When the neighbors found out about it, they were going to kill Gideon, but his father, Joash, said that surely Baal did not need their protection. Gideon then blew a trumpet, and all the surrounding tribes came to him to defeat the Midianites. But God said there were too many there and to send home anybody who would rather not be there. A bunch left, but they were still too many, and Gideon was ordered to watch them drink at the river. Those who lay down and lapped like a dog were sent home. Those who raised the water to their mouth with their hand were retained (were these the more watchful and careful ones?). Then Gideon ordered each of them to bring an earthen pot with a flaming torch inside it. In the middle of the night, they came on the Midianite camp, and every man smashed his pot and held up his torch. The Midianites were already fearful, for they had heard terrible tales of what the Lord had done to other heathen nations. So with the sudden noise and flaring lights, they lost their nerve, ran away, and got killed in the process. This was the typical way battles ended in ancient times (the first to panic lost and were slaughtered as they ran away).

Comment

1 Like many miraculous battle stories, this one makes sense. The battle plan required precise following of instructions, easier with a smaller, more disciplined, and more committed force. Also, the Midianites were already fearful with stories circulating about the defeats the Israelite God had inflicted on other nations. The sudden tumult and flaming lights in the middle of the night threw them into confusion, and they fled.

2 The story is one more example of God's way of dealing with problems. He chooses a person, in this case Gideon, to be his agent to fix things. And in our case that means he calls you and me. If we feel up to it, we probably do not appreciate the magnitude of the task. We must trust God to go with us, point the way, support our efforts, bring us through, and eventually give success. Gladys Aylward was a housemaid with very little education who felt called by God to go as a missionary to China. Every missionary society, one by one, rejected her, but eventually she found her way to China and became particularly involved with the care of unwanted little girls. In those troubled times, with war and disaster all around, she had to take her flock of little girls to safety, and she did. The story was told in the movie *The Little Woman* (she was small in stature but big in heart and faith); it is an inspiring story of what God can do with "ordinary" people.

3 But what about Gideon asking, as Moses before him had done, for signs to convince him that God was really with him? Old-timers called this "putting out the fleece." Jesus said we were not to put the Lord our God to the proof, but he does want us to be convinced in our own minds and will surely help us to become so.

4 The big lesson in all these stories in the book of the Judges is that it is easy to sink into the ways of society around us. The ark must float in the water, but if the water gets into the ark, it sinks. Christians must learn to live in a society and culture that is increasingly adverse or even hostile to Christ and his church. But we must retain our distinctive Christian ways of thinking and acting or we will surely become useless, sink, and eventually disappear.

5 The good news is that God is not willing for this to happen. Christ has promised that the gates of death will not prevail against us. He will send his servants to call us back and establish us in the right way again. You and I are his servants, inadequate as we are.

The Call of Samuel

1 Samuel 1–4

Elkanah had two wives: Peninnah, who had children; and Hannah, his favorite, who had none. Every year they went up to Shiloh to sacrifice to the Lord, and Peninnah taunted Hannah, who went into the temple weeping bitterly and praying fervently. Old Eli, the priest, saw her mumbling to herself and thought she was drunk. Han-

nah told him she was making a vow to the Lord that if he would grant her a child, she would dedicate the child to the Lord. Eli thereupon prayed that the Lord would grant her petition, which he did. When the child, Samuel ("named or marked out for God"), was weaned, she brought him to the temple at Shiloh and left him there with Eli. Presumably, there were women in the place to care for him, and, being so young, he probably did not feel abandoned but accepted his new home. But his mother visited him every year and brought him a new ephod (a sort of priestly apron).

One evening when he was sleeping beside the ark, he heard a voice calling his name. He thought it was Eli, who told him to go back to bed. But when the voice came a third time, Eli realized it was the Lord who was calling Samuel. He told the boy that if the voice came again to say, "Speak, Lord; your servant is listening." The Lord did call him again and entrusted Samuel with a rather hard message to Eli: that his family would be destroyed and replaced by a more worthy line of priests.

Samuel judged (led) Israel for about forty years and held them together both as a nation and as a people loyal to God. Just before Samuel died, he called the people together and challenged them to show if he had at any time taken a bribe or otherwise taken advantage of his position. They could not name one example; he had clean hands, which is more than can be said for a lot of leaders, then and since.

Comment

1 It is interesting that Samuel's sons, like those of Eli before him, did not walk in his ways and were not able to follow him. The same has been true of many other great men, including mighty ministers of the gospel. Why is this? Were these godly men not as good in their home life as they should have been? Were they too much absent from the home? Or is it the tendency of one generation to rebel against the previous one? Who knows? But the problem has more to do with the children than the parents. The converse is also true: that mighty men and women have often been followed by even mightier children. All of us could recite many examples of this. Whether they are mighty or not, it is one of the greatest blessings that any parents can have that their children are in the faith and devoting their lives to the service of the Lord and his needy children.

2 Preacher's kids are often notorious as bad examples, but I think that this is just another example of the exception proving the rule. We are more likely to notice the bad eggs than the good ones. The late reverend Eric Gallagher, a mighty man by any standards, had a famous children's address where he held up a large sheet of paper with an ink blot on it and asked the children what it was. Most answered that it was an ink blot, ignoring the fact that the little blot was surrounded by a huge expanse of clean paper. A good point well made.

David and Goliath

1 Samuel 17

The Philistine army was camped on a hill on one side of the Valley of Elah while the Israelite forces were on the hill on the opposite side. Every morning and evening, Goliath, a huge man (nine feet tall?), came out and challenged any Israelite champion to fight with him. The deal was that if he won, the Israelites would serve the Philistines; if Goliath was killed, the Philistines would serve the Israelites.

All were afraid of him, except David, who had come to bring supplies to his brothers (and cheeses for their captain) and offered to fight him. Everybody laughed at the boy, but when he told King Saul he had killed a lion and a bear in hand-to-hand combat, they took him seriously.

Saul offered him his armor, but it was clumsy. Goliath mocked him for coming against him with a stick like a dog, and he cursed him, using the names of his gods. But David trusted in the living God (the rest were just idols) and laid him out with a stone from his sling and cut off his head with

Goliath's own sword (quite a feat for a lad since it was very heavy). The Philistines did not keep their part of the bargain but fled and were pursued and slaughtered. Saul would not allow David to go home but made him a captain in his army. David was successful there, which aroused Saul's jealousy. The story from then on took a downward turn.

Comment

1 The story of David and Goliath has been told in other places, including the Quran, and has become a favorite, almost proverbial tale, representing little people battling against much greater opponents. The measurements of Goliath, his height and his equipment, vary somewhat in the several accounts of the story, but he was obviously a big one and apparently a representative of a whole family of gigantic warriors, some of whom had six fingers and six toes, clearly genetic monstrosities. A similar nine-foot-tall man is buried in the border country of Scotland. Goliath was called a "champion," which is the translation of a Hebrew term meaning "middleman," who stood out between two armies and challenged someone to come out and engage him in single combat, the fight to determine the outcome in the whole battle. This was a common proceeding then and in later times. Caesar's *Gallic Wars* describe a Roman soldier fighting and killing a huge Gallic champion in similar circumstances.

2 Later, in the time of the prophet Elisha, his attendant had risen early and gone out to discover that an army with horses and chariots had encircled the city. The servant ran back in and said to Elisha, "'Oh no, my lord! What shall we do?' the servant asked. 'Don't be afraid, the prophet answered. 'Those who are with us are more than those who are with them.' And Elisha prayed, 'Open his eyes, LORD, so that he may see.' Then the LORD opened the servant's eyes, and he looked and saw the hills full of horses and chariots of fire all around Elisha" (2 Kgs 6:15-17). In similar perilous situations the message is still the same: We need to open our eyes and see that the resources we have with God on our side are greater than those of our enemies.

3 The story of David and Goliath has inspired the church in many desperate situations. It was cited when the church was suffering and being crushed by the might of the Roman Empire; in the thirteenth century when the Ottoman Turks were threatening to invade and wipe out European civilization, including Christianity: when the church was being persecuted by the Nazis in Germany or the Communists in Russia; in Muslim lands today where they are being crushed

and threatened with extinction. Is their only hope Western military support? The story of David and Goliath would argue otherwise.

4 Following persecution, the faithful church not only survives but revives. Following the end of the Julian persecution, when the Christian bishops were traveling toward Nicea for the great conference there (many of them lacking fingers and toes), people poured out to greet them, asking to be baptized. The same thing has happened since. The blood of the martyrs is the seed of the church. At the height of an earlier persecution, John the seer, a chained prisoner in a cave on the island of Patmos, saw a great multitude whom no man could number out of all nations and tribes and tongues praising God and the Lamb.

5 Even in our own country we still have great enemies, secular forces with mighty armors and weapons that we cannot possibly match. The message of David and Goliath is not to be afraid of them, nor to try to match their equipment and armor and the kinds of weapons that they use, but to meet them in the name of the Lord. Our battle is spiritual, and our weapons are not earthly. God is able to make us mighty in our weakness.

King Saul: Great Start, Poor Finish

The Israelites were not doing very well against their surrounding enemies, who seemed much better equipped and organized for battle than they were. They ascribed this to the fact that their enemies had kings who led them in battle. So they came to Samuel and asked him to appoint them a king such as their neighbors had. Samuel was appalled and asked them had they ever had any king but their God who had led them to triumph against all their enemies. But they insisted. Samuel went and complained to God, who told him to accede to their request and anoint Saul, son of Kish, as their king. Saul did not particularly want to be king and hid among the baggage, but they hauled him out and anointed him king. Most people approved but some worthless people said, "Who is Saul that he should deliver us?"

Shortly after that, Nahash, king of the Ammonites, surrounded Jabesh-Gilead and proposed as a condition of peace that he would put out every man's right eye. The inhabitants of Jabesh-Gilead sent a message to Saul asking for help and said to Nahash, "Give us one day to seek help, and if it does not come by tomorrow, then do whatever seems good to you." When he got their message, Saul was angry, so cut up an ox and sent the parts throughout Israel with the message that this is what would happen to the cattle of anyone who did not show up with him to fight at Jabesh-Gilead. They came in droves and he scattered the Ammonites. Everyone then said, "Let's take care of those nasty people who muttered against Saul." But Saul said, "This is a day of rejoicing in Israel, for we have been saved from our enemies; it is not a time for taking care of old scores." Following this great beginning Saul became too big for his boots and started to take sole charge of things, contrary to the ways God had instructed Samuel. Eventually, God took the kingdom away from Saul and anointed David in his place. Things then started to go very badly for Saul, and an evil spirit entered his heart so that he became insanely jealous of David and tried to kill him several times. David escaped but had to flee for his life and become virtually a bandit chief in the wilderness.

Comment

1 Saul was tall and impressive looking, every inch a king. He was brave and decisive in his actions and made an impressive start in his reign. He was also generous in his strength, and he refused to punish the nasty people who had sneered at him when he first became king. But as commonly happens in such circumstances, success seems to have gone to his head, and he began to act peremptorily and to do whatever seemed okay by him.

2 It is said that an evil spirit entered into him. He became moody and jealous, paranoid even, and David had to flee for his life into the wilderness. It is to David's great credit that while Saul was hunting him down to kill him, he did not take umbrage at this but respected the fact that God had anointed Saul king. When Saul was delivered into his hand, he spared his life, and later when a foreign soldier in Saul's army reported to David (falsely) that he had killed Saul, expecting a reward, David had him put to death for lifting his hand against the Lord's anointed.

3 Saul was always looking for ways to control David and had the great idea of marrying him to one of his daughters, Michal. But unfortunately she fell in love with David and saved his life on at least one occasion when her father had planned to murder him. Saul's son Jonathan likewise formed a lasting friendship with David and saved his life several times by letting David know Saul's plans. Jonathan seemed to be a soulmate for David, being brave and generous and generally a fine fellow. He and David swore an oath together to the effect that when David became king, he would spare Jonathan's family, a promise David kept.

4 The rock bottom in Saul's career came when on the eve of a great battle with the Philistines and no longer on speaking terms with the Lord, he found a witch (forbidden in Israel) and got her to raise Samuel from the grave to tell him how the battle was going to go. Samuel told him exactly how badly things were going to be both for Israel and for Saul's household. The next day in a great battle on Mount Gilboa, Saul and his sons died. Saul fell on his own sword to avoid being made sport of by the Philistines if they captured him. When he heard the news, David mourned not only for his friend Jonathan but also for his enemy Saul and wrote a famous psalm (quoted in 2 Sam 1:13ff.).

Elijah and the Prophets of Baal

1 Kings 18

There had been a sore famine on the land for three years, and at the end of that time, God told Elijah to order King Ahab to meet with him. Elijah called on Obadiah, the steward of Ahab's household, and told him to summon Ahab for a conference. Obadiah was at first afraid to do so, but eventually he complied. When Ahab saw Elijah, he said, "Are you the one who is troubling Israel?" Elijah gave him a short answer, making it clear to Ahab who had really been troubling Israel. Elijah then told Ahab to meet with him on Mount Carmel, on the northwest coast of Israel (neutral or even Baalite territory), and to bring with him all the prophets of Baal for a showdown. This was to decide who was truly God, Jehovah or Baal, the Caananite deity that Queen Jezebel and all Israel were then worshiping.

The rules for the contest were agreed upon, and it was decided that whoever answered by fire was the true God. Elijah gave the prophets of Baal the first roll of the dice. They set up their altar and called on Baal from morning until evening, chanting and dancing and even cutting themselves with knives, but there was no answer. Elijah taunted them, saying, "Shout louder; maybe he is having a nap or is gone on a journey somewhere." Eventually, the prophets of Baal were exhausted and gave up.

At the time of the evening sacrifice, Elijah took twelve stones (representing the twelve tribes of Israel), built an altar, and laid wood on it with the sacrificial animal on top. Then, to make the trial more convincing, he poured four large barrels of water on the sacrifice three times until it overflowed and filled the trench he had dug around it. Then he prayed: "Lord God, let it be known this day that you are God in Israel and that I am your servant and have done these things as you have commanded me and that you are turning the hearts of your people back." Fire came down from heaven and consumed the sacrifice and licked up all the water. When the people saw it, they said, "The Lord, he is God; he is God."

Elijah slew all the prophets of Baal by the brook Kishon. Elijah then went up to the top of Mount Carmel and cast himself down and told his servant to look toward the sea. The servant said, "I see a little cloud, a mere hand breadth." Elijah told him to look again as the skies darkened with an approaching rain storm. The drought was over, and God was back again with his people. Ahab got into his chariot to return to his capital city Samaria before the road got flooded, and Elijah was so excited that he ran alongside the chariot and kept up with it.

Comment

1 It would seem that Elijah had won a mighty victory over the forces of the evil idol Baal, that the Israelites had seen that their God JHWH was the real God, and that they would return to their covenant with him that had been confirmed under Moses and Joshua and Samuel. But if you think this is the end of the story, you are sadly mistaken. The mighty victory was swiftly followed by a mighty defeat—for Elijah and apparently for God too. This indeed was not the end but only the beginning of a new and quite different story.

The Terrible Queen Jezebel

1 Kings 19

With the great victory on Mount Carmel, Elijah and Ahab thought it was all over. But they had not taken Queen Jezebel into account. When Ahab told her what Elijah had done to her prophets, she said, "The gods do so to me and more also if I make not his life as one of theirs before this time tomorrow." Faced by the wrath of this terrible woman, Ahab backed down, and Elijah fled. He journeyed into the wilderness and lay down exhausted under a juniper tree and prayed that he might die. But an angel supplied him with food and water, and he continued his journey for forty days to Horeb, the mountain of God, and took up residence in a cave.

But God spoke to him and said, "What are you doing here, Elijah?" Elijah replied, "I have been zealous for the Lord, but the people have broken their covenant with God, torn down his altars, and killed his prophets with the sword. I alone am left, and they are seeking my life to take it away." Then God told Elijah to go and stand in the mouth of the cave while the Lord passed by. There was a mighty wind that shattered the rocks, but God was not in the wind, then a consuming fire, but God was not in the fire. Finally, there was a "still small voice." That was God, and he told Elijah to do three things: to anoint Jehu king of Israel, replacing Ahab; to appoint Hazael king over the Syrians in Damascus; and to appoint his servant, Elisha, to be the prophet of God in his place.

Comment

1 This is a turning point in the history of God's people. Mount Horeb is another name for Mount Sinai (there were several names for it), where Moses received the Law with earthquakes, fire, and storms. But times were changing. God is about to guide his people differently and to a more definite end, the coming of his son, the Messiah. The persecutions of Jezebel had created a faithful nucleus within Israel so that a new and greater Israel was emerging and the plan of salvation was about to move into a higher gear. God is now going to be seen in events of history: the replacement of King Ahab by Jehu; the setting up of Hazael as king of Israel's neighbor Syria; the work of Elijah's successor, Elisha. And so far from Elijah being the sole remaining loyal Israelite, he is told that there are seven thousand in Israel

who have never bowed the knee to Baal. There will be from then on a new and different generation of prophets who are going to raise up and prepare a loyal core of people. This will be a new and greater Israel, who will be able to receive and understand the Messiah, fulfilling the promise to Abraham that in him and in his seed all the families of the earth would be blessed, not Israel alone. These new prophets spoke of a God concerned about righteousness (see Mic 6:8). They would foretell the coming of the Messiah, describing exactly the sort of person he would be—not a mighty warrior defeating their enemies, but a savior, the Lamb of God who would take away the sin of the world (see Isa 53).

2 This story tells us never to be pessimistic about the world or the church. Elijah thought that all was lost and that he was the only loyal soul left, but he was wrong. We must always remember that God is at work, often silently in the background but nonetheless powerfully. And just when we think all is lost, a mighty new expression of God's power and gracious will suddenly appears. The Wesleyan revival was a good example of this. Everything in England appeared to be going down the tube when suddenly God was powerfully at work in the land and in the world. We should always be sure that God is active even when appearances argue otherwise. Evil movements and empires seem irresistible and unstoppable, but they are built on sand, so they fold up and disappear. But those founded on the rock survive and emerge again, and good things happen. The darkest hour is often just before dawn.

Jonah and the Whale

Jonah 1–4

Jonah was a prophet, and the Lord told him to go and preach against Nineveh, the great capital of the cruel Assyrian Empire. But he did not want to go there, for they were his deadly enemies, so he tried to flee from the presence of the Lord. He got into a ship in Joppa (on the coast of Palestine) and set sail for Tarshish, a city in southern Spain, then considered the far end of the world. But a great storm arose, and the crew, fearing for their lives, cast lots to see who was the sinner for whose crimes this storm had come upon them. The lot fell on Jonah, and he advised them to throw him into the sea, which they did, whereupon the storm ceased.

However, God did not let Jonah drown but prepared a great fish (not a whale), which swallowed him. He lived in its belly for three days. There, he repented and cried to the Lord, who heard him, and the fish vomited him up on the beach. He went to Nineveh and told them that in forty days God was going to destroy the city. The inhabitants, including the king, repented and cried to the Lord, and he heard them and did not destroy them. Jonah was angry about this and went and sulked under the shelter of a gourd outside the city. But a worm killed the gourd, and Jonah was again very sorry at the loss of his shelter from the heat of the sun. But God said, "Why are you sorry about the gourd and have no pity for the inhabitants of Nineveh?"

Comment

1 This is a favorite Bible story, almost as famous as Noah and the ark and David and Goliath, but there are serious problems if we take it literally. There is no known fish that could swallow Jonah whole, though I am sure such a monster could be found somewhere. But how could Jonah survive in the stomach acid and digestive juices of the monster, not to mention breathe? The story has all the marks of a parable and is better taken that way.

2 It is a wonderful message about how we should think about and treat our enemies, even deadly ones. We should pray for them and do so with hope, for God loves them too, as he did the cruel Assyrians, and he can speak where we cannot and accomplish what is beyond our powers.

3 God has done so in our time. The Japanese military code seemed unshakably militaristic even after the war, but Japanese culture has shied away from that altogether. The same can be said about German militarism, and though the Russians are strutting around a bit, it is unlikely that they will wish, in Nikita Khrushchev's terms, to bury us. We need to see the invisible armies of the Lord and know that the tide of battle is not always to the strong, for the Lord of battles is ultimately in charge, invisible but still almighty.

4 There are other kinds of enemies, cultural forces that would like to marginalize or even outlaw Christ and his church. They are busy in our own society, and like the Philistines of King David's day, they threaten us. We must stand and fight, always remembering, however, that the battle is spiritual, not political, and that we have the resources of heaven on our side.

5 What do we wish for our enemies? Not their humiliation and defeat and destruction, but their coming to a better frame of mind, as happened with Jonah's enemies, the Assyrians. And this too has happened in our time. We have seen the provisional IRA, responsible for many crimes and cruelties, come round and seek to move forward, cooperating with those whom they had formerly hated (and who hated them). Many of the terrorists, in both camps, have come to real Christian faith. We should indeed, as St. Paul advised us in 1 Corinthians 13, always be hopeful, patient, abounding in the work of the Lord. This is not to say that we should not take measures to protect ourselves, but we should constantly be aware that these measures, though necessary, are not the whole answer.

The Call of the Prophet Isaiah

Isaiah 6

Isaiah, son of Amoz, was a prophet in the southern kingdom (Judah) during the eighth century BC. His activity covered the reigns of five kings of Judah. He wrote and published his prophecies, which are preserved in the book of Isaiah. The first five chapters are a summary or general outline of his prophecies (well worth reading). In chapter six he gives an account of his call to be a prophet. He dates this call to the year that King Uzziah died. This was a disastrous event to the people of Judah, for Uzziah had been an exemplary king, and things had gone well with Judah during his reign. Now, with Uzziah gone and much less worthy kings in his place, things were going to pot. In addition, or perhaps because of this, Judah was threatened by great powers, especially Assyria, and needed a steady hand at the helm to survive.

But in that very year, when the hearts of all were failing, Isaiah had a vision. He saw the Lord (Adonai) high and lifted up, and even the very hem of his robe filled the temple. Around him stood the seraphim, an order of angels with six wings (the really important angels had no wings at all and the cherubim only two). With two they covered their faces; with two they covered their feet; and with two they flew. And they cried, "Holy, holy, holy is the Lord of hosts; the whole earth is filled with his glory." The glory of God (shekinah) had filled the temple of Solomon, but the temple was too small for God, and his glory filled the whole earth. The foundations of the temple shook at the voice of the one who cried (these were huge stones that supported the pillars of the temple), and the house was filled with smoke (one of the ways in which God's presence was made known). And Isaiah said, "Woe is me; I am doomed, for I am a man of unclean lips, and I live among a people of unclean lips, for my eyes have seen the king, the Lord of hosts." But one of the seraphim took a burning coal from the altar with a pair of tongs and touched his lips with it, saying, "Now that this has touched your lips, your iniquity is taken away, and your sin purged." Then Isaiah heard a voice saying, "Who shall I send, and who will go for us?" He replied, "Here am I. Send me."

Comment

1 What is a prophet, and how is a prophet called? The answer of the Bible is that a prophet is one who listens to God and declares his will to others. The prophets of old often told of forthcoming events, but this is not necessarily so, or at least not in the way we like to think of foretelling the future. Indeed, the Lord's people are all called to be prophets in the sense that they declare God's will to those around them. We are seldom called on to predict the future, for we are seldom sure what it may bring (man proposes, but God disposes), and we are accustomed to being surprised at the way things turn out, commonly quite differently and often much better than we had hoped. But we must speak out in the name of God when things are definitely wrong and when a word from God needs to be heard. And one word that we are sure is true and must be proclaimed with everything we have is that Jesus is the Son of God and the savior of all who call on him.

2 We have a tendency to think too optimistically about our moral condition—to think that, all things considered, we are not too bad. The great corrective of this is to see the holiness of God. Isaiah saw this in a symbolic vision. We can see it in the life and teachings of Jesus. The bar is very high indeed. However, God can put a new heart in us so that we want to serve him with our whole heart. But this does not mean we feel good about ourselves. Especially when we are looking at the words and deeds of Jesus, all our righteousness seems like filthy rags, and we are glad to throw ourselves down before a merciful God who can touch our lips, make us clean, and forgive all our sins and shortcomings and give us the desire to be different.

3 Thus positioned, fear and uncertainty vanish. We are ready to say "Here am I," to follow Christ and deal with whatever comes along. St. Paul said, "I have learned how to get by on little and to be glad when I have enough. I can do all things with Christ who strengthens me."

Isaiah's Prophecy of a Return to Zion

Isaiah 35

The desert and the parched land will be glad;
    the wilderness will rejoice and blossom.
Like the crocus, it will burst into bloom;
    it will rejoice greatly and shout for joy.
The glory of Lebanon will be given to it,
    the splendor of Carmel and Sharon;
they will see the glory of the LORD,
    the splendor of our God. (vv. 1-2)

Read through the chapter in your Bible.

Comment

1 This is the prophetic promise to the Jews in exile that God was not through with them. They would return again—not all of them, but a faithful remnant, purified and refined by their captivity.

2 Inspired by our merciful God, this might be a good time to think about the displaced people of the earth, those driven from their homes by wars and terrorism. We would hope that they can be provided with homes in the West and that they may be able, sometime in the future, to return to their own homes.

3 We should also remember those whose entire lives have been destroyed by natural disasters.

4 We should remember those families whose working members have become unemployed.

5 Finally, we should remember those families at the bottom of the heap, where children go to bed hungry.

6 And let us not only ask God to help them but to tell us what part he wishes us to play in his plans for their relief.

Isaiah: The Promise of the Messiah

Isaiah 53

Who has believed our message
and to whom has the arm of the LORD been revealed?
He grew up before him like a tender shoot,
and like a root out of dry ground.
He had no beauty or majesty to attract us to him,
nothing in his appearance that we should desire him. (vv. 1-2)

Read through the chapter in your Bible.

See also Isaiah 7:14: *"Therefore the Lord himself will give you a sign: The virgin will conceive and give birth to a son, and will call him Immanuel."*

Comment

1 These two passages have been interpreted as a prophecy by Isaiah of the coming Messiah. Other interpreters, especially those who are Jewish, hold that the prophet was referring to a reborn Israel, not a personal messiah. But the passages are remarkable, describing with great accuracy and attention to detail the events of Jesus' life, mission, character, and way of life. The idea that his suffering is an offering for sin is also present.

2 This prophecy brings to mind Jesus' entry into Jerusalem in the last week of his life, seated upon a donkey, the symbol of a king coming in peace. He was proclaiming, or rather acting out, who he was in a dramatic manner. The crowds sang, "Hosanna to the Son of David," clearly indicating their belief that he was the Messiah. When the Jewish rulers asked him to tell his followers to desist, he replied that if they did, the very stones would cry out (Luke 19:40).

3 We can hardly be expected to know exactly what was in the mind of the prophet when he spoke these amazing words, but even assuming that he was not actually thinking of the coming of Jesus, he must at least have been saying more than he knew. It remains a remarkable prophecy.

4 This passage has been made more familiar to us by Handel's *Messiah*, especially by the beautiful recitative, "Surely he has borne our griefs and carried our sorrows." Indeed, this entire passage, often referred to as the song of the suffering servant of the Lord, simply puts into beautiful poetic form the whole doctrine of the atoning death of Christ, ransoming us from sin and death

Hosea: The Pursuing Love of God

Hosea was a contemporary of Amos in the eighth century BC, but he prophesied in the southern kingdom of Judah. He was particularly concerned with the growth of idolatry among his countrymen, picking up heathen ideas and practices from their surrounding neighbors in the course of business and with whom they were intermarried. Hosea married Gomer, a prostitute. It is not certain whether this was in the ordinary way of love and marriage, or whether he deliberately married Gomer to

graphically illustrate his message (like Jeremiah purchasing a plot of land at a time when you could hardly give it away, Jer 52:7).

Gomer was continually unfaithful to Hosea, running after lovers who gave her rich presents. They had two children, who Hosea named Lo-Ruhamah ("not loved") and Lo-Ammi ("not my people"). But when her lovers abandoned Gomer, Hosea kept buying her back from slavery and reinstating her as his wife. He used his life experiences to demonstrate the unfailing and persistent love of God for his unfaithful people. They will end up in a wilderness with the loss of all their gains and all their false hopes. Gomer, losing all her rich presents and having been abandoned, will eventually remember the early days of her marriage (like the early days of Israel with God and Moses) as the good times, and she will return to her husband, who will receive her gladly.

Although Hosea pronounces judgment on the northern kingdom, Israel, which he says will be carried away into captivity, Judah, for the moment anyway, will be spared. Ultimately, Hosea is a hopeful prophet. Just as he continued to love and redeem Gomer, so the Lord will persist in his concern for his people and bring them back from captivity. Hosea even promises that God will reunite Israel and Judah under one ruler. How has this promise been fulfilled?

Comment

1 Often, we are tempted to despair about the state of the church. In the "good times," when the church was prospering and people largely attended worship, we complained about the mere formality and poor quality of their devotion. Now, in harder times we complain about their ungodliness, their abandonment of the church. We need to remember Christ's promise that the church would never die. The "good times" should not make us complacent, and the hard times should be seen as God's efforts to winnow and purify the church, bringing us back to a deeper commitment to do God's will and be his people. Remember how Elijah complained that he was the only true Israelite left, but God told him that there were in Israel seven thousand who had never bowed the knee to Baal. Pessimism is never well founded, and undue optimism isn't good either.

2 The learned Bishop Butler (1692–1752) was invited to be considered as Archbishop of Canterbury. He declined, saying that he did not wish to officiate at the funeral of his church. Yet at that very time God was preparing for the great revival of true religion associated with the Wesleys. Many instances of the same kind of unexpected revival of hope could be cited. They are still happening.

3 This unexpected change of fortune can also be mirrored in our own lives when unexpected blessing is found amid disaster and well-founded hope replaces despair.

4 This hopefulness should also extend to our enemies and those who seem to be hopelessly committed to evil. Terrorists have become transformed into good and useful people by the grace of God, and we need to pray for them in faith and hope. Remember Jonah, who could not imagine the terrible Assyrians repenting. But they did.

The Prophet Amos:
Religion without a Caring Heart

Amos was a shepherd and a cultivator of sycamore figs, a large and nutritious variety of fig much prized in the Middle East. Sycamores produced better fruit with good attention, which apparently included beating them at a certain stage of development. Amos was insistent that he was neither a prophet nor a prophet's son, distinguishing himself from the sons of the prophets who had become professional soothsayers and whose messages were designed to suit the expectations of their listeners (see 2 Kgs 22:11).

Amos and the great prophets who followed him took their authority from the call of God and only proclaimed what they heard from him. Amos, a southerner, was ordered to go to the northern kingdom, Israel, to the religious centers of Bethel and Samaria, and declare to them a coming "day of the Lord," which was going to destroy them for their wickedness and see them carried off into a strange land.

The eighth century BC was a time when things were going well for the nation of Israel. Jeroboam II had conquered most of the small kingdoms surrounding Israel and extended its boundaries to match those of the days of Solomon, and a period of peace and great wealth followed. But this was not ultimately good, for in these prosperous times the wealthier, pushing business, exploited the poor to the point that they were sold into slavery for even small debts (the righteous were sold for a pair of sandals). The wealthy and prosperous, however, were very assiduous in their religious observances, seeking God's favor (and in some cases the favor of heathen gods as well). They were even looking forward to the "day of the Lord," when a blessed time for all would come on the land.

Amos told them that the day of the Lord would be darkness, not light, and that they would be smitten by pestilence, famine, and the sword, taken away into captivity. Needless to say, this message did not go down well with the priests in Bethel and the rulers in Israel generally. Amaziah, the priest at Bethel, complained to King Jeroboam about Amos and ordered him to go back to Judah, his own country, and prophesy there. He apparently was forced to do so, and we learn from other sources that since he was forbidden to speak, he committed his words into writing so they could be read. Those who should know say that his writings are remarkable both for their clarity and style. He was the first prophet to do so, and all the prophets who came after Amos, especially Isaiah, Jeremiah, and Ezekiel, also wrote down their words, which are preserved for us in the Bible.

Comment

1 The great prophets were not appointed by kings or priests or by anybody else, but directly by God, and this continues into our own times. We recognize God's call to people to become ministers, but we do not call them; God does. And we are all called to be prophets, listening to God speaking to us and acting as he commands us. We, like them, have the inner voice of God speaking within our hearts, and we also have something Amos and the others never had: the written scriptures, telling us God's word for us.

2 Perhaps the most important part of Amos's message for us is that religiosity is not necessarily a good thing, and may even be offensive to God. God wants obedience, not ceremonial offerings. Building up the structures and organizations of the church is not necessarily pleasing to God. Amos's message to the ultra-religious but morally bankrupt Israelites was to "let judgment run down like water and righteousness like a mighty stream" (Amos 5:24). We are judged by our works, not by outward observances. True religion always shows itself in actions, not in words and ceremonies. Note the energetic lives of the Wesleys and their followers in the social degradation and horror of eighteenth-century England.

3 But the best part of Amos's prophecy is a message of hope. He keeps pleading with the Israelites to change their minds and their ways, promising that if they did so, God would be gracious to them. Further, after all the troubles that were about to descend on them, God would lead a faithful remnant back to their own land and restore them into their proper place in his plans for the salvation of mankind. All this holds for the church today.

Ezekiel: The Valley of Dry Bones

Ezekiel 37:1-14

The hand of the LORD was on me, and he brought me out by the Spirit of the LORD and set me in the middle of a valley; it was full of bones. He led me back and forth among them, and I saw a great many bones on the floor of the valley, bones that were very dry. He asked me, "Son of man, can these bones live?"

I said, "Sovereign LORD, you alone know." (vv. 1-3)

Read through verse 14 in your Bible.

Comment

1 Ezekiel, like the prophets before him, had neither a pleasant task nor an easy life. He was carried into Babylon in the first captivity of the Jews and called

and appointed by God to be a prophet to a people who appeared to have learned nothing by their troubles. They continued to worship idols, the gods of their Babylonian neighbors. Ezekiel was instructed by God to bring messages of doom one after the other, but nobody paid any attention to him. His calls to repentance fell on deaf ears. When those who had been left behind in the land of Israel continued in their evil ways, Jerusalem was besieged by a Babylonian army and fell, followed by a second deportation of the people to Babylon. At this point Ezekiel's message changed, and he began to prophesy doom to their enemies and became a prophet of hope to his people, who were now scattered through many nations with their morale at zero. In chapter 27 of his book, Ezekiel brings a great message of hope in the vision of the valley of dry bones, restoring the glories of King David's reign to them.

2 Some have interpreted this vision literally as meaning that the Jews will recover their home in Palestine. Indeed, the flow of Jews back into Palestine and the establishment of the state of Israel seemed to be the beginning of the fulfillment of that hope. But as the great Dr. Beet constantly reminded us, prophecy and the fulfillment of prophecy are two different things, and we may fail to recognize it when it comes.

3 But the message of Ezekiel is a great word of encouragement to the church in our time. As we look on the Christian church in our own land and throughout the world, it is easy to become discouraged in the present and fearful of the future. But God is not dead. The mighty whirling chariots envisioned by Ezekiel are still around us, and though God works quietly and (for our taste) rather slowly, his chariots still move, swerving neither to the right nor to the left but straight on. Our business is to be faithful and courageous, knowing that God is at work as Ezekiel saw in his vision.

Jeremiah: The Prophecy of a New Heart

Jeremiah 24

After Jehoiachin son of Jehoiakim king of Judah and the officials, the skilled workers and the artisans of Judah were carried into exile from Jerusalem to Babylon by Nebuchadnezzar king of Babylon, the LORD showed me two baskets of figs placed in front of the temple of the LORD. One basket had very good figs, like those that ripen early; the other basket had very bad figs, so bad they could not be eaten.

Then the LORD asked me, "What do you see, Jeremiah?"

"Figs," I answered. "The good ones are very good, but the bad ones are so bad they cannot be eaten."

Then the word of the LORD came to me: "This is what the LORD, the God of Israel, says: 'Like these good figs, I regard as good the exiles from Judah, whom I sent away from this place to the land of the Babylonians. My eyes will watch over them for their good, and I will bring them back to this land. I will build them up and not tear them down; I will plant them and not uproot them. I will give them a heart to know me, that I am the LORD. They will be my people, and I will be their God, for they will return to me with all their heart.

"'But like the bad figs, which are so bad they cannot be eaten,' says the LORD,

'so will I deal with Zedekiah king of Judah, his officials and the survivors from Jerusalem, whether they remain in this land or live in Egypt. I will make them abhorrent and an offense to all the kingdoms of the earth, a reproach and a by-word, a curse and an object of ridicule, wherever I banish them. I will send the sword, famine and plague against them until they are destroyed from the land I gave to them and their ancestors.'"

Comment

1 Jeremiah is known as the weeping prophet. He is credited with the book of Lamentations and generally had bad news for his people. Unlike Amos, who was an obscure shepherd in the desert regions of Tekoa, he came from an influential family in Jerusalem. They were the priests of Anathoth. He was not a willing prophet. Like Moses, he claimed he could not speak and was just like a child, but God told him he would put words into his mouth and be like an iron fortress around him to protect him from his enemies. He needed this protection because everybody hated him for his dismal message. The southern kingdom, Judah, was to be transported to Babylon just as had happened to the northern kingdom, Israel, which had been scattered by Assyria. People reacted violently to this message. His own kin, the priests of Anathoth, tried to have him killed, but since the plot was discovered, he was delivered from their hand. A temple official, Pashur, had him beaten and put in a muddy well to starve to death, but friendly officials told the king, who had him drawn out and imprisoned instead in the palace. Jeremiah used living parables to bring home his message. He walked around with a yoke on his neck to graphically show the future bondage of his people. A false prophet, Hananiah, took the yoke from him and broke it to indicate that there would be no bondage. Jeremiah complained to God about all this hard usage and tried to stop prophesying, but the message, he said, was a like a fire in his bones, and he had to keep delivering it to his hostile people. He was released from imprisonment by the Babylonians and apparently ended his days in Egypt.

2 Jeremiah's message was not all doom. He also prophesied that a faithful remnant would develop in exile and, purified from the sins of their fathers, would return to rebuild Jerusalem. This would not be an outward matter. Rather, it would be a return to keeping the Law of Moses literally, as in the days of King Josiah, for God would rewrite the law in their hearts, an inward renewal.

3 This religion of the heart is Jeremiah's great message. The heart in the Bible is not just a pump. It is used to represent our most inward and true being; it is where we really live. As a man thinks in his, heart so is he (Prov 23:7). Likewise, St. Paul says that circumcision, the mark of God, is in the heart, not the flesh (Rom 2:29). One of John Wesley's standard sermons, the walking theology of the Methodists, is titled "The Circumcision of the Heart."

4 God's salvation is not a reform; it is a new creation. Only God can rewrite the message on our hearts. We do not need to be repaired; we need to be remanufactured. It is like being born all over again, and God promises to perform this miracle in our hearts if we open them to him. And since it is a miracle, you can't pull it out and look at it. It is a mystery. In John 3, it is said to be like the wind: you can hear it, but you can't see it, nor do you know where it is coming from or where it is going. So is every one that is born of the Spirit.

The Patience of Job

Job 1

One day the angels came to present themselves before the LORD, and Satan also came with them. The LORD said to Satan, "Where have you come from?"

Satan answered the LORD, "From roaming throughout the earth, going back and forth on it."

Then the LORD said to Satan, "Have you considered my servant Job? There is no one on earth like him; he is blameless and upright, a man who fears God and shuns evil." (vv. 6-8)

Read Job 1 in your Bible.

Comment

1 First, a follow-up note from the Bible. These disasters would be enough to try anyone's faith, but there was more to come. Job developed a horrible skin disease, so bad that he had to scrape the debris off his skin with a piece of broken pottery. But in all this, though he cursed the day he was born, he never said a word of complaint about God. When his three friends came to "comfort" him, they assured him that he must have sinned secretly and also greatly to have caused God to bring such suffering upon him. They exhorted Job to confess his sin, whatever it was, and repent so that God could end his misery. Job rejected their assumptions vehemently and wanted to appear before God to plead his case and find out why all these evils had come upon him.

2 I remember well how, as a beginning Christian, I took up the book of Job and read it, hoping to find the answer to my questions about suffering. I also remember my disappointment when I failed to find any answers whatsoever to my questions in the book of Job.

3 Job simply sits down and shuts up when he finally meets with God. Stephen Fry, a well-known actor and author, is a prominent atheist. In a recent interview he was asked what he would say to God if it turned out that he was wrong. He responded immediately, "Bone cancer in children." To him and many others, this negates the possibility of God's existence. What has the book of Job to say to Stephen Fry and others like him who find that unmerited suffering and the idea

of God do not mix? The first point to note is that the book of Job is not so silent on the matter as it might seem. The difficulty with Stephen Fry's argument is that in getting rid of one problem, they run foul of another and a worse one—namely, explaining the universe as an accidental occurrence. Job's answer is not as blindfolded as it might appear. Having seen God, he was certain an answer existed even though he could not see it at the time.

4. The logical form behind atheistic arguments citing undeserved suffering focuses on the evidence that appears to be contrary to belief in God, which therefore demonstrates that he does not exist. However, they are back with Aristotle's model of reasoning, so-called *vertical logic*, which starts with a supposedly true proposition and argues down through the evidence to deduce an equally true conclusion. If we fail in our argument, the initial proposition is shown to be false. Any adverse evidence casts doubt on the initial premise. This proceeding is a recipe for doubt and confusion. Modern linguistic logics, based on game theory, provide a better method, comparing possible explanations side by side to see which fares best. Almost any theory you can imagine, scientific or otherwise, including the big bang, has problems, but provided the big bang is a better fit than the alternatives, it will, in Charles S. Pierce's terms, justify reliance (i.e., belief). In other words Job's position, for all its continuing problems, is justifiable. Having seen God and believed in him, he knows the answer is in there somewhere.

5. But there is something more to be said. In fact, there is quite a bit to be said for God's inclusion of "bad" things in his creation.

   a. The winnowing features of the animal world are part of a wonderful system, so much more interesting than a pain-free machine. It has become apparent in recent years, as biological systems have been studied more carefully, that predation is an essential condition not only for the functioning of the system but for the health and well-being of the prey animals. Even the trees and vegetation are affected. Overgrazing would be one explanation of this, but there are other factors involved. As the predators chase the prey animals, they force them into large groups, which pound the earth. This appears to be essential to the health of the vegetation, so when the predators disappear, the entire system begins to malfunction and deteriorate. It has been found essential to reintroduce wolves into the national parks to improve the health of not only the prey animals but even the trees and vegetation. The disappearance of sharks has likewise been linked to environmental problems in the oceans.

b. It has also become apparent that much of our distaste on seeing nature as "red in tooth and claw" derives from imagining ourselves in a similar situation. But the creatures are not like us in this respect. Birds and deer and prey creatures generally keep a sharp weather eye out for predators, but they do not seem to worry about their situation as we humans would. After the chase and kill they seem to settle down and get on with their lives quite calmly even when the predators are still nearby.

c. There are also interesting mechanisms for mitigating pain in prey animals. I know a gynecologist who studies surgical procedures with sheep (he has a special license to do so). He used spinal anesthesia on his animals so the surgical procedure was painless. The animals had to be firmly held in position while he injected the anesthetic dugs into their spinal fluid, and he noticed that when so immobilized, they did not respond to the needle in their back as they normally would. He concluded that immobilization produced an anesthetic condition. If he is correct, and he confirmed this finding over and over again, it would seem that once a deer or a wild hog is seized by a predator, further happenings are painless. A nice little bit of thoughtfulness is built into the system.

d. There are also many more appealing things built into the system. There is heroic self-sacrifice on the part of parents and even fellow members of the group. A mother rabbit will attack a stoat in defense of her young, and deer will attack and chase away leopards and hyenas in the same circumstances. Herd and other group animals, such as elephants and lions, show great concern not only for their own young but for other members of the group.

e. With regard to human suffering, there is also much to be said in favor of theodicy.

    i. Would a world where there was no uncertainty, nothing to fear, and where nothing bad could happen to us really be better for us than the dangerous and uncertain world we know? This might be so if God were growing vegetables, but he is growing children, planning to take them into his family business. We grow and mature most in response to hardship rather than in the easy parts of our experience. The physician/poet John Keats, who died of tuberculosis at the age of twenty-six in London, saw much horrible disease in the fever epidemics that spread into the city from the colonies, and he came to view disasters as a means of developing the divine possibilities of our nature. He described this life as "the vale of Soul-making."

ii. Likewise, the great earthquakes and tsunamis and volcanic eruptions that destroy lives and homes draw us together and stir us up to help one another in unselfish and indeed sacrificial ways. Any natural disaster area becomes a hive of activity from all around the world as people, especially Christians, move to help the afflicted.

iii. With regard to allowing the wickedness and cruelty inflicted on the weak and helpless, especially the young, what would we have God do about it? On the one hand, if he punished wrongdoing immediately, this would certainly get rid of the problem but would make us virtually machines, where we would not behave well but really not behave at all, only react positively to a strong compulsive environment. On the other hand, not to respond to wickedness at all does not sound like good government but rather no government at all. The world as the Bible presents it to us has a compromise between these two extremes: God works, but works silently as Jesus told us. The rule of God shows itself like a crop in the field, growing silently and slowly but inexorably (Luke 17:20). Evil carries its own reward, as does good. The first psalm expresses this well. The good are like a tree planted by the water; its leaves do not wither, and whatever it does will prosper. But the evil are not so; what they do will eventually be blown away like dust in the wind. Henry Wadsworth Longfellow, in his poem "Retribution," wrote, "Though the mills of God grind slowly; / Yet they grind exceeding small; / Though with patience He stands waiting, / With exactness grinds He all."

f. And nature, the great backdrop to the grand opera of human existence, reflects these same principles. It is not an easy world, but one where undesirable things are weeded out; where kindness is present but not obvious; where the wonders of God are displayed with intricate systems of great beauty that speak eloquently of God but do not do so in our face.

Daniel in the Den of Lions

Daniel 6

It pleased Darius to appoint 120 satraps to rule throughout the kingdom, with three administrators over them, one of whom was Daniel. The satraps were made accountable to them so that the king might not suffer loss. Now Daniel so distinguished himself among the administrators and the satraps by his exceptional qualities that the king planned to set him over the whole kingdom. At this, the administrators and the satraps tried to find grounds for charges against Daniel in his conduct of government affairs, but they were unable to do so. They could find no corruption in him, because he was trustworthy and neither corrupt nor negligent. Finally these men said, "We will never find any basis for charges against this man Daniel unless it has something to do with the law of his God." (vv. 1-5)

Read Daniel 6 in your Bible.

Comment

1 The book of Daniel is considered prophecy in the English Bible, but it is classed among the "writings" (*kethuvim*) in the Masoretic Bible, where it is considered a form of literature rather than a historical account. It is therefore usually dated in the era of the persecution of the Jews in the time of Judas Maccabaeus and his family (167–160 BC) rather than in the sixth century BC, the Persian era. It may, of course, be based on traditions deriving from a more ancient source. The basic theme of the book is God's protection of his people in a time of dire persecution.

2 The book's value as scripture is by no means lessened by this figurative understanding. The basic message of the story, and of the three loyal Hebrews in the fiery furnace, is that God protects and preserves his own. But this is not to be understood in a simple way so that we will always escape. God cannot operate like that; his hand must not be so obvious. He has to work quietly and not force himself on everybody's attention so that everyone would be more or less compelled to get into line. God's people have had to go into the lions' den and through the fires of persecution, and they were often maimed or died there. Of course, these things, as St. Paul tells us, are nothing compared with the joy set before us. Nevertheless, God moves in these situations in several ways for our benefit and

to further his cause. St. Paul said that he glories in tribulation (Rom 5:3) and so we should. In the first place he may indeed rescue us either by circumstances or by the instrumentalities of other people. Paul was rescued many times. But the sacrifice is never wasted. God's cause is forwarded in the event. God used the cruel martyrdom of the deacon Stephen (Acts 7) to convert Paul from enemy to apostle.

3 The word *martyr* (*marturos* in Greek) means "witness," and how we conduct ourselves in desperate circumstances is a powerful witness to oppressors and bystanders alike. Daniel's behavior in this situation influenced King Darius, turning him toward God. The calm behavior of the Moravian children in a storm that threatened to sink the ship was a powerful influence on John Wesley, leading him on to become God's evangelist in the horrible eighteenth century. The attitude of the Christian martyrs in the Muslim lands is bound to work on the minds both of their murderers and also the bystanders. The blood of the martyrs is the seed of the church.

4 Our behavior not only in life-threatening times but in the general exigencies and trials of life, small and large, is a most important part of our witness to our Lord and savior and undoubtedly one of the most powerful forms of evangelism that exists. The daily practice of the presence of God that Brother Lawrence, the lowly monk, demonstrated in the kitchen of the Dominican monastery of Paris is important for us and also for those around us.

Nebuchadnezzar's Golden Image

Daniel 3

King Nebuchadnezzar made an image of gold, sixty cubits high and six cubits wide, and set it up on the plain of Dura in the province of Babylon. He then summoned the satraps, prefects, governors, advisers, treasurers, judges, magistrates and all the other provincial officials to come to the dedication of the image he had set up. So the satraps, prefects, governors, advisers, treasurers, judges, magistrates and all the other provincial officials assembled for the dedication of the image that King Nebuchadnezzar had set up, and they stood before it. (vv. 1-3)

Read Daniel 3 in your Bible.

Comment

1 The meaning of this story is similar to that in the previous story of Daniel in the lions' den, a story of God's protection in times of disaster. The comments are much the same, with one exception. When the three loyal Hebrews were commanded by the king to worship the golden image or perish in the burning fiery furnace, they replied that their God would save them, but if not, they would still refuse to worship the heathen image.

2 Christians during times of persecution are not required or even advised to seek martyrdom; if persecuted in one city, they are instructed by Jesus himself to flee to the next (Matt 10:23).

3 If push comes to shove, we are expected to stand by our faith as the three Hebrews Shadrach, Meshach, and Abednego did. Various Christian groups in the recent troubles in the Middle East were offered mercy if they would convert to Islam. Few, if any, did, choosing to suffer death with Christ rather than deny him. In the second century the friendly city officials begged the beloved Polycarp, bishop of Smyrna, to pour out a little wine to the divine emperor and no harm done. He refused, saying, "These eighty and two years have I served him, and he has never done me any harm. Shall I now deny my Christ?" He was burned to death at the stake.

4 Jesus said, "Whoever acknowledges me before others, I will also acknowledge before my Father in heaven. But whoever disowns me before others, I will disown before my Father in heaven" (Matt 10:32-33). St. Paul reiterates this warning (2 Tim 2:12).

5 The same principle holds not only when we are faced with major persecution but also when we are tempted to be silent about our faith. We do not have to run around shouting that we are Christians, but we must always be prepared to make it known that we are Christians. We acknowledge whose we are and whom we serve.

6 Finally, our attitudes toward hardships and troubles of lesser force are important. As we endure hardships and minor disasters in the practice of the presence of God, we are martyrs in the sense of being effective witnesses to the power of Christ.

The Humbling of King Nebuchadnezzar

Daniel 4

"This is the dream that I, King Nebuchadnezzar, had. Now, Belteshazzar, tell me what it means, for none of the wise men in my kingdom can interpret it for me. But you can, because the spirit of the holy gods is in you." (v. 18)

Read Daniel 4 in your Bible.

Comment

1 Babylonian records, unlike those of the Assyrians, do not go into details about the mighty deeds of their rulers, but some such episode may indeed have happened to King Nebuchadnezzar. The strange madness, though rare, is known and is called boanthropy, where the individual believes he is an ox and behaves accordingly. Unlike Nebuchadnezzar's illness, however, it is usually fatal.

2 This is not a message for suffering humanity but for insufferable rulers who see themselves as being in command and make plans for their own aggrandizement. However, there are other forms of self-love, equally bad or worse, among ordinary people who make plans for their own advantage and benefit.

3 This is the empire-building syndrome, fueled by powerful position and directed to personal aggrandizement, and it has many expressions, small and large, from the Napoleons and Hitlers of this world to the minister of the Ballysloughguttery Methodist Church planning to build a new sanctuary. It is the sin of the inhabitants of the plain of Shinar (Gen 11), who said, "Let us build a tower reaching up to heaven and make a name for ourselves." It is in fact the old sin of pride that appeared in the garden of Eden, seeing what we can do on our own without God. There are a couple of old stories that are fitting commentaries on this theme:

- A celebrated organist was giving a concert featuring Bach's music and announced from the organ, "I will now play Bach's Toccata and Fugue in D minor". He struck the keys, but there was no sound. Then the little urchin who pumped the organ appeared around the corner of the organ loft and announced, "*We* will now play Bach's Toccata and Fugue in D minor." Point made: We accomplish very little on our own, and we will accomplish nothing of lasting good without God. God opposes the proud and exalts the humble (Prov 29:23).

- The second old story on the opposite tack concerns a minister who was admiring a garden and said to the gardener, "It is wonderful what you and God have done together here." The gardener replied, "You should have seen it when God had it on his own." God has left a great deal of the management of things, in the earth and the church and just about everywhere else, to his children. We are God's coworkers, and we must do our part.

Wisdom Literature

Proverbs and Ecclesiastes

"Like a gold ring in a pig's snout is a beautiful woman who shows no discretion."—Proverbs 11:22

The book of proverbs is all about wisdom. It is also about fools and foolishness. The Eskimos have numerous words for snow, and the Israelites had multiple words for fools. One of the bad names was nabal. You may remember the prosperous sheep farmer of that name who rudely refused to give David some supplies for his men in recognition of the protection that David had provided for his flocks and shepherds. He was only saved from the complete destruction of his entire operation by the intervention of his wise wife, Abigail (see 1 Sam 25).

But what is wisdom? It is not just learning or absorbing information. It is making use of knowledge for good ends. The fool is quoted as saying in his heart, "There is no God." Note where he said it—in his heart, not just in his head. He was directing his path in an unwise direction, which would lead to misery and ruin. Think of some other things that were considered foolish by the Wisdom writers.

Booze: *"Wine is a mocker and beer a brawler; whoever is led astray by them is not wise" (Prov 20:1).*

Sexual immorality: *"For the lips of the adulterous woman drip honey, and her speech is smoother than oil" (Prov 5:3).*

Deceitful practices: *"Who winks maliciously with his eye, signals with his feet and motions with his fingers" (Prov 6:13).*

Keeping bad company: *"Do not answer a fool according to his folly, or you yourself will be just like him" (Prov 26:4).*

Avoid them: *"Better to meet a bear robbed of her cubs than a fool bent on folly" (Prov 17:12).*

Laziness: *"Go to the ant, you sluggard; consider its ways and be wise!" (Prov 6:6).*

"How long will you lie there, you sluggard? When will you get up from your sleep?" (Prov 6:9).

Wisdom and godliness: *"The fear of the LORD is the beginning of wisdom" (Prov 9:10).*

Comment

1 What do we make of all this wisdom? Is it simply worldly wisdom—that if you do well, you will prosper, and vice versa? Hardly. It is godly wisdom. Frances and I have often noted how our parents, with little formal education, were so wise in ordering their lives, meeting its problems, and advising others in their troubles. And it came from their faith. They did not just remember words from the Bible; the Bible was in their hearts and minds, in their very bones, and it made them wise.

2 Charles Wesley wrote a lovely hymn based on the wisdom of the book of Proverbs, "Happy the Man That Finds the Grace":

Happy the man that finds the grace,

The blessing of God's chosen race,

The wisdom coming from above,

The faith that sweetly works by love.

Wisdom divine! Who tells the price

Of wisdom's costly merchandise

Wisdom to silver we prefer,

And gold is dross compared to her.

Happy the man who wisdom gains,

Thrice happy who his guest retains!

He owns, and shall for ever own,

Wisdom, and Christ, and heaven are one.

The Psalms

Read Psalms 1; 8; 19; 23; 34

Comment

1 The psalms (or songs) were sung in Israel by choirs of musicians in the tabernacle (and later in the temple). Many of them are ascribed to David, but there are several psalmists (e.g., Ps 90, which is ascribed to Moses). A great many of the psalms are complaints to God or urgent requests for God to do something about the psalmist's troubles, especially to take care of their enemies. These mean little to us in our more ordinary moods but can be meaningful in times of great trouble or despair: "Why, my soul, are you downcast? Why so disturbed within me? Put your hope in God" (Ps 43:5).

2 Most of the psalms speak to our hearts and call us to praise God. Some are especial favorites. Psalm 1 is an obvious choice: A godly person is described as a tree planted by the river with deep roots, well-nourished and bound to bring forth fruit in due season, whereas the ungodly, being rootless, are like chaff, which is blown away by the wind.

3 Psalm 23 is another favorite: David, himself a shepherd and later the shepherd to the nation of Israel, reflects on his life and concludes that the Lord has been his shepherd through difficult and dangerous times. In the latter part of the psalm, he also feels that his life with God has been like a feast in his honor, with his cup filled full and running over and the oil of welcome poured on his head.

4 Even in adversity the Christian can bear testimony to these blessings. David knew a lot about adversity, for he was chased throughout his life by King Saul and had to seek sanctuary with the king of Gath, an old enemy. His life hung by a thread during all those days. He was also betrayed by people he had helped. The inhabitants of a city he had rescued from the Philistines sent word to King Saul and offered to hand David over to him with certain death following. Later, his own son, Absalom, rebelled, and David had to flee across the river Jordan to the desert to avoid being murdered.

5 Psalms 8 and 19 are also particularly meaningful to us today: David, who must have often gazed and marveled at the sky, sees the sun and the stars like a great choir, praising God day and night, a book that everyone can read and so learn of God's glory. How much more would David have marveled if he had known what

modern science and space exploration have shown us about the vastness of the universe and its mathematical nature?

6 Psalm 34 is another great one: The psalmist, remembering all God's goodness to him and help in time of trouble, bursts forth, saying, "I will extol the LORD at all times; his praise will always be on my lips" (v. 1). We could go on listing favorite after favorite with the psalmist inviting us to join with him in praising and exalting God.

7 We should not leave the psalms without mentioning the penitential psalms, in which David asks for God's mercy following his terrible moral fall, where a moment's indulgence led step by step to adultery and the murder of his loyal friend Uriah the Hittite. We may not have committed adultery and murder, but we all need God's mercy.

8 The psalms were the hymnbook of Israel and continued as a main part of Christian worship. In the synagogues they were chanted joyfully in Hebrew. In the medieval church and in modern churches in the Anglican and Catholic tradition, they are still chanted in plainsong using translations of the original words. The Scottish psalter took a different line, rendering the psalms into metrical verse, often taking great liberties with the English language. The old-time Presbyterians even thought that it was sacrilege to sing the psalms outside solemn worship, so they used silly rhymes about the mouse and the clock for use in choir practice. But many of the metrical psalms rose to great heights and became firm favorites, including the following:

> O Magnify the Lord with me
> With me exalt his name
> When in distress to him I called
> He to my rescue came....
>
> Fear Him ye saints and you will then
> Have nothing else to fear
> Make you His service your delight
> He'll make your wants his care.

Some major hymn writers have also weighed in on the psalms. The most famous of these is probably Henry W. Baker's version of Psalm 23, "The King of Love My Shepherd Is."

9 We will end this brief presentation of the psalms with the advice to commit your favorites to memory. They will lift your spirits in times of joy and comfort and strengthen you in times of sorrow. Even the cursing psalms may come into play when some act of horrible cruelty comes to your notice—hopefully along with an added prayer for the perpetrator's repentance and salvation. Such mighty changes of heart happen, probably more often than we would expect.

The Story of Ruth

Ruth 1

In the days when the judges ruled, there was a famine in the land. So a man from Bethlehem in Judah, together with his wife and two sons, went to live for a while in the country of Moab. The man's name was Elimelek, his wife's name was Naomi, and the names of his two sons were Mahlon and Kilion. They were Ephrathites from Bethlehem, Judah. And they went to Moab and lived there.

Now Elimelek, Naomi's husband, died, and she was left with her two sons. They married Moabite women, one named Orpah and the other Ruth. After they had lived there about ten years, both Mahlon and Kilion also died, and Naomi was left without her two sons and her husband. (vv. 1-5)

Read through verse 18 in your Bible.

Comment

1 And now for the rest of the story: Ruth and Naomi went to Bethlehem, the family seat, and sought help from Boaz, a near relative. Ruth followed the reapers in the harvest field and picked up what they left behind, as the Law provided. Boaz noticed Ruth and instructed the reapers to leave a little extra for her. Naomi took this as a favorable omen and instructed Ruth to lie down beside Boaz where the harvesters slept on the floor and to uncover his feet (a sign of her claim for help from a relative, according to the Law). Boaz then had the duty to marry her and raise up children for her deceased husband. He was more than willing to do this, especially since Ruth impressed him as a very good woman for looking after her mother-in-law. But there was a closer relative who had a prior right, and Boaz met with him in the gate of the city, the usual place where business was conducted, and offered him the right to marry Ruth. He declined the honor, so Boaz married her, and she became the great-grandmother of King David.

2 This is a lovely story of family loyalty—and a love story at that—but it is more. The Moabites were the deadly enemies of the Israelites. Their religion involved the sacrifice of little children, which was called "the abomination of Moab" by the Israelites. One exception here was that the king of Moab sheltered David's parents when Saul was hunting him down in the wilderness. But when David sent messengers to console his son, the current king of Moab, on the death

of his father, the Moabites grossly insulted them, shaving their hair off and sending them home half-naked (David almost exterminated them for that). Yet here is a Moabite woman being held up as an example of goodness and being identified as the great-grandmother of King David. This should have been a disgrace, but instead it is celebrated.

3 So why was this story told and included in the Hebrew Bible among the writings (*kethuvim*)? Like the story of Jonah, it is telling the people of God to love their enemies. Jesus told us, "Love your enemies and pray for those who persecute you, that you may be children of your Father in heaven. He causes his sun to rise on the evil and the good, and sends rain on the righteous and the unrighteous" (Matt 5:44-45).

Part 2
New Testament

The Birth of Jesus: The Wise Men

Matthew 2

After Jesus was born in Bethlehem in Judea, during the time of King Herod, Magi from the east came to Jerusalem and asked, "Where is the one who has been born king of the Jews? We saw his star when it rose and have come to worship him."

When King Herod heard this he was disturbed, and all Jerusalem with him. When he had called together all the people's chief priests and teachers of the law, he asked them where the Messiah was to be born. "In Bethlehem in Judea," they replied, "for this is what the prophet has written:

"'But you, Bethlehem, in the land of Judah,
        are by no means least among the rulers of Judah;
    for out of you will come a ruler
            who will shepherd my people Israel.'"

Then Herod called the Magi secretly and found out from them the exact time the star had appeared. He sent them to Bethlehem and said, "Go and search carefully for the child. As soon as you find him, report to me, so that I too may go and worship him."

After they had heard the king, they went on their way, and the star they had seen when it rose went ahead of them until it stopped over the place where the child was. When they saw the star, they were overjoyed. On coming to the house, they saw the child with his mother Mary, and they bowed down and worshiped him. Then they opened their treasures and presented him with gifts of gold, frankincense and myrrh. And having been warned in a dream not to go back to Herod, they returned to their country by another route. (vv. 1-12)

Comment

1 The story of the three wise men is a prominent part of the Christmas celebrations in Christian churches. It features in plays and Christmas cards and in all sorts of ways. It is generally taken to be a nice little story but most unlikely to be true. It has also been pointed out that it is only mentioned in the Gospel of Matthew. Matthew was an apostle and a Gospel writer, representing in general the traditions of the Jerusalem church. Luke, who told about the angel visitation to the shepherds, would have had available to him eyewitnesses and perhaps even written accounts of the birth of Jesus, which, according to St. Luke, abounded.

2 There is also an interesting account in chapter 11 of *The Travels of Marco Polo*, which records his finding of the tomb of the Magi (a translation of a Persian word for a Zoroastrian priest) inscribed with their traditional names, Balthasar, Caspar, and Melchior. He also recorded information about their ages, their status, and the reasons for their gifts: gold for a king, frankincense for a God (or priest), and myrrh for a healer. Since the child's parents accepted their gifts on his behalf, this confirmed to them that he was all three: king, God, and healer. They are recorded to have become believers on their return to Persia and to have established Christian worship there. Marco Polo also identified a group of fire worshipers in a nearby castle, who represented the church that the wise men established. The tradition there gives the reason for the connection with fire. It seems that the parents of the baby Jesus, in return for their gifts, gave the wise men a stone (a common religious gift such as Jews lay on the tomb of a close relative or friend). The Magi at first thought nothing of the gift and allegedly threw it down a well, but fire is supposed to have come down from heaven into the well. They preserved and transported that flame home with them and distributed it to every Christian place of worship they established.

3 Modern studies of the story are also instructive. I imagined as a child that the star moved ahead of the wise men from the East until eventually it stopped over the manger in Bethlehem, which would indeed have been a miraculous occurrence. But that is not what the Bible story says. The wise men saw the wonderful star in the East and, being astrologers, interpreted it to mean that a king was to be born among the Jews. So they traveled to Jerusalem, reasonably expecting to find the future king there. They would have been informed there that the Messiah was expected to be born in Bethlehem, so they traveled on there, and the wonderful star appeared again.

4 What was this remarkable star? All sorts of explanations have been put forward, but the most plausible one is that of the great seventeenth-century astronomer Johannes Kepler, who opined that it was a convergence of Jupiter, Saturn, and Mars lining up behind one another. Those particular planets would have provided them with the interpretation of the occurrence. One such convergence appeared in October in 8 BC and the second in April the next year, which would have been visible in Bethlehem. I was always puzzled that the star stopped over Bethlehem, but the planets are always moving very slowly. They reach their zenith and reverse their movement, at which point they appear to be stopped.

5 Maybe we should get the story of the Magi off the Christmas cards and into our minds and join them in the worship of the king.

The Birth of Jesus: The Shepherds

Luke 2:8-17

And there were shepherds living out in the fields nearby, keeping watch over their flocks at night. An angel of the Lord appeared to them, and the glory of the Lord shone around them, and they were terrified. But the angel said to them, "Do not be afraid. I bring you good news that will cause great joy for all the people. Today in the town of David a Savior has been born to you; he is the Messiah, the Lord. This will be a sign to you: You will find a baby wrapped in cloths and lying in a manger." (vv. 8-12)

Read through verse 17 in your Bible.

Comment

1 The date of Jesus' birth is disputed. According to Luke the census took place when Quirinius was governor of Syria, which took place in AD 6. In Matthew's Gospel Herod was still alive, which would put the date around 8 BC, a date consistent with the conjunction theory about the star of Bethlehem. But fixing dates in early times is always a chancy business as records are not always reliable.

2 The story of the angels and the heavenly choir is another favorite story on cards and in church plays and pageants during the Christmas season. As such, it seems more like a nice story than a real event. But the announcing of the birth of the Savior to the shepherds in advance of anyone else (Mary and a few others excepted) makes sense. To us, shepherds bring to our minds favorable images: David, the shepherd boy who watched over Israel as king; and Jesus, the good shepherd. But at the time of the nativity, shepherds were at the bottom of both the social and economic heap. They were anathema to respectable Jewish people, as they could not keep the Sabbath or attend services. Also their occupation did not attract the better sort of people, for it was not an appealing job, being out in all weathers, day and night, and from time to time it was dangerous, having to ward off wolves or bears trying to carry off lambs. So only those who were not able to find anything better would take the job. Their reputation for bravery and honesty was, not surprisingly, questionable. Jesus described the hireling who did not care about the sheep running off when a wolf appeared (John 19:12). One Jewish proverb said that you might as well make your son a thief as a shepherd. In short, the arrival of the long-awaited Messiah was announced not only to the wise (the Magi) but also to the scum of society. God's message of salvation is always aimed particularly at the outcasts. Jesus was criticized for associating with the despised, such as prostitutes and tax collectors. St. Paul reminded his church members,

"Not many of you were wise by human standards; not many were influential; not many were of noble birth.... God chose the lowly things of this world and the despised things—and the things that are not—to nullify the things that are" (1 Cor 1:26, 28). The bottom rungs of our own society are well populated, and we need to continually remember them, as God did, and especially at the Christmas season.

3 The chorus of the angel host is also appropriate. For the biggest event in human history, nothing less than a vast choir of angels would have been adequate for the overture.

4 The message of the angel song is peace, for the promised Messiah is the Prince of Peace who brings this divine gift to mankind. When the risen Jesus entered the upper room with the fearful disciples, he said, "Peace be unto you." Peace in the Bible is not merely the absence of war but genuine harmony and reconciliation of the parties. So Christ brings peace in our hearts, so we are at peace with ourselves, with those around us, and with God.

5 However, the arrival of the king does not bring peace for everyone. Many will not want to hear of it. The identity of those who will receive the peace mentioned in the angel's song has been variously translated. The AV calls them just people. Other versions calls them people of good will. Others speak of them as "those to whom he is well disposed"—in short the chosen ones of God, the elect. The peace of God then is not a general peace but rather the peace that exists even in the middle of a storm. Jesus said, "Peace I leave with you; my peace I give you. I do not give to you as the world gives" (John 14:27). The world can neither give nor take away this peace from us.

Luke 2:39-52

When Joseph and Mary had done everything required by the Law of the Lord, they returned to Galilee to their own town of Nazareth. And the child grew and became strong; he was filled with wisdom, and the grace of God was on him. (vv. 39-40)

Read through the chapter in your Bible.

Comment

1 We know little or nothing about Jesus' infancy. We are told that he grew, waxed strong in spirit, was filled with wisdom, and that the grace of God was upon him. When he was around twelve years old, conversing with the teachers of the Law, we are told that he grew in wisdom and stature and was generally well

regarded. The Monophysite Christians (claiming that Jesus had only one nature and that it was divine) were an early heresy. They taught that Jesus, even as an infant, was God, upholding the universe even when he was in his mother's arms. Some hymns and Christmas cards suggest the same thing. However, the Bible, though it says very little about Jesus' infancy and childhood, does not support this. There is no mention of anything other than what one would expect from a perfectly normal baby with normal childhood and development. Luke's Gospel only states that the grace of God was with him. His discussions with the teachers of the Law depict a normal conversation, only that these graybeards were astonished by both his questions and his answers. His baptism by John the Baptist seems to have been an important occasion when he was affirmed as God's beloved Son; from then on he acted and appeared as the Son of God and Messiah.

2 The temptations in the wilderness followed. These were temptations to use his authority and power to bring in the kingdom of God quickly. So he might, for openers, feed the starving populace or perform spectacular miracles so that everyone would believe in him. Or he might seize political power to make the nations obey him and so put everything right. All these he rejected, quoting scripture, and chose instead the way of the cross.

3 The transfiguration on the mountain (mentioned in the Gospels and also by Peter in his first letter) must have confirmed to him, and certainly to the three chosen disciples who accompanied him, that he was the divine Son of God. But immediately following this, he began to warn the disciples that his path was not to earthly victory and glory, the way they thought of the Messiah, but to humble obedience and divine sacrifice.

4 He identified himself as Messiah by teaching miracles associated with the messianic hope: the lame walk, the blind see, and the poor have the good news preached to them. However, most of these and other miraculous signs he accomplished by prayer to the Father (e.g., the raising of Lazarus from the dead, John 11).

5 In short, as the great creeds put it, he was fully human and fully divine—the two combined together in a single person without division, in perfect harmony.

6 This is the incarnation, described in the first chapter of St. John's Gospel, where "the Word became flesh and made his dwelling among us. We have seen his glory, the glory of the one and only Son, who came from the Father, full

of grace and truth" (1:14). This idea that God's Son could be incorporated into a baby boggles the imagination. We can represent it with words, but like many things, natural and divine, it is beyond our powers of imagination. We have every reason to believe that it is so, but we cannot imagine it. It is, in the theological sense, a mystery.

The Wedding in Cana of Galilee

John 2:1-12

On the third day a wedding took place at Cana in Galilee. Jesus' mother was there, and Jesus and his disciples had also been invited to the wedding. When the wine was gone, Jesus' mother said to him, "They have no more wine."

"Woman, why do you involve me?" Jesus replied. "My hour has not yet come."

His mother said to the servants, "Do whatever he tells you."

Nearby stood six stone water jars, the kind used by the Jews for ceremonial washing, each holding from twenty to thirty gallons.

Jesus said to the servants, "Fill the jars with water"; so they filled them to the brim.

Then he told them, "Now draw some out and take it to the master of the banquet."

They did so, and the master of the banquet tasted the water that had been turned into wine. He did not realize where it had come from, though the servants who had drawn the water knew. Then he called the bridegroom aside and said, "Everyone brings out the choice wine first and then the cheaper wine after the guests have had too much to drink; but you have saved the best till now."

What Jesus did here in Cana of Galilee was the first of the signs through which he revealed his glory; and his disciples believed in him.

After this he went down to Capernaum with his mother and brothers and his disciples. There they stayed for a few days.

Comment

1 Drunkenness was a serious public disgrace and generally avoided by respectable Jews. They (and the Greeks too) commonly mixed their wine liberally with water. They did use wine but mostly to flavor and sanitize their water, which was often of doubtful quality. The advice in the book of Proverbs is not to look on the wine when it is red. This is because that is the color of undiluted wine. Indeed, the book of Proverbs has a great deal to say about wine, mostly precautionary. But at a wedding things might have been loosened up a bit.

2 The occasion of this miracle was an embarrassing one for the bridal couple. They had run out of wine at the bridal feast. Jesus' mother appears to have been a sort of marriage director for the occasion, and for whatever reasons, she stepped up to the plate and tried to repair the situation. She knew well by then who Jesus was, and it immediately occurred to her that he could do something about this social disaster, so she ignored his demurral and told the servants, "Do whatever he tells you to do." Jesus, as always, was reluctant to use his influence and powers in a public display, but he knew the situation and ordered the servants to fill the six twenty-gallon jars with water and then to bring some to the governor of the festivities (master of ceremonies). He tasted it and found it, as we would expect, to be of top quality.

3 The comment of the governor of the feast on the wine has become a byword among experienced Christians, for they say it means that Jesus always keeps the best wine to the last. Many good things become better and better as we get older. This is true of the Christian life. The old chorus says that "every day with Jesus is sweeter than the day before." It is also true of a good marriage. If it is not true of our work, it is usually because we have the wrong motivation for our

daily occupation. Financial success and professional success are heady benefits, but they do not satisfy for long. When we start a new career, we worry about whether or not we will be able to make a living and whether we will be a success or a miserable failure or somewhere in between. But this only sustains us for a few years, if that long; we have to feel that we are doing good. Many a difficult or even miserable job has become rewarding when we feel we are filling a slot and doing good. And the more you feel you are doing good, either at the work itself or to the people you meet with in your work, the more rewarding your working life will be, and it will probably continue to get better. I know some people with difficult and demanding jobs who are reluctant to retire. God wants to bless us in every way—in our life, in our home, and even in our daily work.

The Adulterous Woman

John 8:2-11

At dawn he appeared again in the temple courts, where all the people gathered around him, and he sat down to teach them. The teachers of the law and the Pharisees brought in a woman caught in adultery. They made her stand before the group and said to Jesus, "Teacher, this woman was caught in the act of adultery. In the Law Moses commanded us to stone such women. Now what do you say?" They were using this question as a trap, in order to have a basis for accusing him.

But Jesus bent down and started to write on the ground with his finger. When they kept on questioning him, he straightened up and said to them, "Let any one of you who is without sin be the first to throw a stone at her." Again he stooped down and wrote on the ground.

At this, those who heard began to go away one at a time, the older ones first, until only Jesus was left, with the woman still standing there. Jesus straightened up and asked her, "Woman, where are they? Has no one condemned you?"

"No one, sir," she said.

"Then neither do I condemn you," Jesus declared. "Go now and leave your life of sin."

Comment

1 This story is not found in any of the early Greek manuscripts, but few, other than some hypercritical scholars, doubt that it was a genuine event in Jesus' ministry. It rings true. It is contained in Codex Bezae (the main Western

manuscript used to prepare the authorized version of the Bible) and was included by Jerome in his Vulgate translation of the Bible. It was therefore accepted as genuine by the Council of Trent. It is also interesting that Codex Sinaiticus, an important fourth-century Greek manuscript, while it omits this story, has a symbol in the margin at the appropriate page, indicating that other manuscripts contain it. It may have been omitted from an earlier manuscript by accident or perhaps by design since offense may have been taken at the kindly approach of Jesus to an adulteress.

2 The story itself is odd. Both parties in adultery were to be stoned, according to the Law of Moses, and this woman is said to have been taken in the very act. Where, then, was the man? It is likely that the adulterous man was released for cooperating with the authorities in trapping Jesus. If Jesus said "Stone her," he would be in trouble with the Roman authorities. If he said "Don't stone her," he would be in trouble with the Jewish authorities for contradicting the Law of Moses.

3 As usual, Jesus was too much for them. He did not answer the question directly but said someone without sin should cast the first stone. It would take a bold person to take up that challenge, for being guilty of breaking one part of the Law was held to be the same thing as being guilty of all. His words have become a proverbial saying.

4 Jesus then bent down and wrote with his finger in the dust. Nobody really knows what he wrote, though all sorts of suggestions have been put forward. Perhaps he wrote some telling quotation from one of the prophets about mercy being preferred to sacrifice. Why he wrote in the dust is an easier question to answer, as he was probably trying to avoid embarrassing the already shamed woman by discussing the case in her presence.

5 Notice the vast difference between the attitude of the scribes and Pharisees and of Jesus. All they saw was what she had done (and the use they might make of it). They did not give any thought as to how she might be feeling. Jesus looked deeper and saw a troubled and probably abused woman. How did she get into this plight? Did she fall victim to the wiles of a predatory male? Was she driven to it by poverty? Or did she just grow up in a bad home? Whatever the case, Jesus saw that she was not a bad woman, certainly not hopeless, and thoroughly shamed. So he said, "Neither do I condemn thee. Go, and sin no more." And I bet she didn't, not that one anyway.

Jesus Healing on the Sabbath

John 5:1-18

Some time later, Jesus went up to Jerusalem for one of the Jewish festivals. Now there is in Jerusalem near the Sheep Gate a pool, which in Aramaic is called Bethesda and which is surrounded by five covered colonnades. Here a great number of disabled people used to lie—the blind, the lame, the paralyzed. One who was there had been an invalid for thirty-eight years. When Jesus saw him lying there and learned that he had been in this condition for a long time, he asked him, "Do you want to get well?"

"Sir," the invalid replied, "I have no one to help me into the pool when the water is stirred. While I am trying to get in, someone else goes down ahead of me."

Then Jesus said to him, "Get up! Pick up your mat and walk." At once the man was cured; he picked up his mat and walked.

Read through verse 18 in your Bible.

Comment

1 For a long time no evidence existed of a pool by the sheep gate in Jerusalem. Thus, the omniscient critical scholars of the nineteenth century concluded that the fourth Gospel was a late writing. Archaeological excavation, however, has since found the pool exactly where the Gospel located it and, for other considerations (e.g., no mention of the sacking of Jerusalem and the destruction of the temple), have suggested a date for the Gospel of John earlier than AD 70.

2 A more serious question is raised about the common belief at the time that an angel occasionally disturbed the water and the first one into the pool on

that occasion would be miraculously healed. The Gospel does not comment on this belief one way or the other, but the power of suggestion might indeed produce marvelous healings. A massive study of the antidepressant Prozac is a case in point. It was deemed so powerful that depressed people taking it were reported to become hyperactive and even violent and homicidal. The study covered thousands in both the test and placebo groups. It was found that Prozac was indeed an effective antidepressant, but that the placebo was equally helpful. A similar result was found when X-rays were found effective in treating warts. One curious radiologist treated the warts with the sound of the machine working but no radiation being delivered. The results were equally good.

3 The amazing thing about Jesus' healing of this man was that he had not been walking for thirty-eight years. His muscles should have been so wasted that he would hardly be able to walk, if at all, much less carry his bed.

4 The reaction of the religious Jews to this healing makes for sad reading. Here is a man who has been unable to walk for decades, no doubt reduced to beggary (for he had no supporting friends or family) and misery, who is now able to walk about, and they are complaining because he was healed on the Sabbath. There is a good principle behind the idea of a Sabbath rest, but this is carrying it to silly extremes.

John 11

Now a man named Lazarus was sick. He was from Bethany, the village of Mary and her sister Martha. (This Mary, whose brother Lazarus now lay sick, was the same one who poured perfume on the Lord and wiped his feet with her hair.) So the sisters sent word to Jesus, "Lord, the one you love is sick." (vv. 1-3)

Read through verse 53 in your Bible.

Comment

1 The raising of Lazarus from the dead was a great miracle. It was not only an act of mercy and a demonstration of the power of God, but it was also meant to teach something; it was a sign. It is interesting that the miracle was accomplished, like most miracles, by God in answer to prayer. It was wonderful, but it was not magic.

2 This story represents the final teaching on the subject of life after death. Life beyond the grave had a long history in the Old Testament. The ancient Israelites believed the dead lived in a ghostly realm under the earth (*Sheol* in Hebrew). The prophet Samuel was called up from there by the witch of Endor to tell Saul what was to be his fate in the coming battle with the Philistines (Sam 28). It was not thought to be a pleasant place. Later, however, we find the idea that at the last day, the dead would be raised up to be judged by God. Sheol was divided into two parts: The part where the godly dwelt was called "Abraham's bosom" and was a place of joy. It was also called "paradise" after the great pleasure parks of the Persian kings. The other part was a place of torment. This view was prominent in New Testament times and can be found in the parable of the rich man and the beggar Lazarus (Luke 16:19-31).

3 Martha, Lazarus's sister, surmised, "I know my brother will rise again in the resurrection at the last day." Jesus put his stamp on the matter, just as he had on the Law of Moses, saying, "I am the resurrection and the life; he who believes in me shall never perish, and whoever lives and believes in me shall never die."

4 How are we to put all this together? First, we have the view that Jesus still taught: that all rise to be judged by their works on the last day. Then there is this other idea that those who believe in Jesus will not pass into judgment but are already in the presence of God and the angels. We must realize, as the great J. Agar Beet would remind us, that we are speaking of future events and that prophecy and the fulfillment of prophecy are two different things. The Jews expected the Messiah but did not recognize him when he arrived. So we must be cautious and

tentative in interpreting these things. The simplest way to think about them is to say that mankind in general will be judged at the last day by a merciful God, who, knowing all things, can determine where their heart lies and how they would have responded to the great light of the Messiah if they had been given the opportunity. On the other hand, those who have already accepted and believed in the Messiah will not go into judgment with the rest and will not even wait until the last day. Rather, when they die, they will pass directly into the presence of the Lord. Jesus also said, "Very truly I tell you, whoever hears my word and believes him who sent me has eternal life and will not be judged but has crossed over from death to life" (John 5:24).

5 Where does that leave the rest of mankind? It is not for us to know. They are in the hand of a merciful God who always does what is right.

The Story of Zacchaeus: A Social Outcast

Luke 19:1-10

Jesus entered Jericho and was passing through. A man was there by the name of Zacchaeus; he was a chief tax collector and was wealthy. He wanted to see who Jesus was, but because he was short he could not see over the crowd. So he ran ahead and climbed a sycamore-fig tree to see him, since Jesus was coming that way.

When Jesus reached the spot, he looked up and said to him, "Zacchaeus, come down immediately. I must stay at your house today." So he came down at once and welcomed him gladly.

All the people saw this and began to mutter, "He has gone to be the guest of a sinner."

But Zacchaeus stood up and said to the Lord, "Look, Lord! Here and now I give half of my possessions to the poor, and if I have cheated anybody out of anything, I will pay back four times the amount."

Jesus said to him, "Today salvation has come to this house, because this man, too, is a son of Abraham. For the Son of Man came to seek and to save the lost."

Comment

1 This story rings true. The sycamore-fig tree was a common fruit tree that produced quantities of large figs and was much prized and widely cultivated in suitable places in the Middle East, including the Jordan valley and the Jericho region. It was also easy to climb. The character of Zacchaeus also is credible. My father was short, and my mother maintained that short men had a Napoleon complex; they were pushy to compensate for what they perceived as their physical

handicap. It is easy to see how Zacchaeus, taunted in his youth by his peers, would decide to carve his own way to success and, having ability, become the chief tax collector in Jericho, which had a big export business in balsam and other products. His great wealth, however, came at a price; he was regarded as being beyond the pale by his fellow Jews and hopelessly lost by respectable people generally. In turn, he would hate their religion and their values and anything to do with them. In a word, he was a lost soul, despised and hated by all and hating them all in return.

2 But God was not content to leave him that way. Jesus of Nazareth was passing by, and such a notorious figure was worth a peek. He even climbed into a little tree to get a better look at him.

3 This story tells of Jesus' powers. He was truly human and prayed for God's help like anyone else, but he was the beloved Son of God who poured special graces on him, of knowledge and of power. He knew not only that Zacchaeus was in the tree but also knew his name and presumably all about him and the misery of his heart. And the Lord called to him with a better offer than he ever could have imagined.

4 No Jew in his right mind would have gone into Zacchaeus's house. They would not even eat any food that had been touched by his shadow. And they were outraged that Jesus went and stayed with a notorious sinner like Zacchaeus.

5 If Jesus' offer was astounding, Zacchaeus's response was even more so: a complete abandonment of everything he had been and worked for.

6 Jesus' comment says it all. Salvation had come to this house, and this hopeless outcast is miraculously changed. He is now a true Israelite, a child of Abraham, the great man of faith who went out at God's command when he did not even know where he was supposed to go. No repentance could have been more complete. And this is what Jesus desires, total surrender and total compliance.

7 Wouldn't it be nice to know what became of Zacchaeus? As with many characters Jesus met and touched, we are not told. But I bet it would be worth hearing.

8 The offer still stands. We can hear his voice and leave the hovels we have striven to build and the stuff we have accumulated and the iron bands of bad choices we have accumulated, and become free, full members of the family of God, his Children, walking in his way with his blessing resting on all that we are and do.

Jesus and Nicodemus

John 3:1-21

Now there was a Pharisee, a man named Nicodemus who was a member of the Jewish ruling council. He came to Jesus at night and said, "Rabbi, we know that you are a teacher who has come from God. For no one could perform the signs you are doing if God were not with him."

Jesus replied, "Very truly I tell you, no one can see the kingdom of God unless they are born again."

"How can someone be born when they are old?" Nicodemus asked. "Surely they cannot enter a second time into their mother's womb to be born!" (vv. 1-4)

Read through verse 21 in your Bible.

Comment

1 This conversation took place at night because Nicodemus was afraid of what might happen if the Jewish authorities found out he had been talking to Jesus. But Jesus, ever considerate, did not raise this question with him, for he knew that the marvel was not that Nicodemus came at night but that he came at all. It showed that he was thinking along the right lines. Nicodemus's question was a serious one, the most serious that any human being can ask. Essentially, he wanted to know how he should live so that he might gain God's favor and enter his eternal kingdom. John Wesley similarly said, "One thing I want to know, the way to heaven."

2 Why did Jesus' answer puzzle Nicodemus? It was not that he did not know what the expression "born again" meant. It was that he could not see how it applied to him. When a Gentile became a Jew, he had a ceremonial bath to wash off the filth of the Gentiles and then put on clean garments. Starting off life afresh as a totally different creature was called being born again. But if you were born a Jew, this was not necessary. When a young person came to the age of understanding (around thirteen), he would voluntarily take upon himself the responsibilities of being an Israelite in the bar mitzvah ceremony.

3 Jesus' answer, in effect, was that it was not enough to be an Israelite by natural birth; a spiritual change was needed. It was not enough to be born of water, becoming an Israelite, but more importantly of water and of the spirit, becoming a child of God in one's very nature, one's heart.

4 Jesus further explains this mystery by the analogy of the breeze: You can hear it and feel its effects, but it is invisible. So is everyone who is born of the spirit. The change is evident, but the mystery remains. It cannot be seen, only known to have happened from perceived changes in character, outlook, and behavior. Jesus then goes on to say two more things about this great spiritual change:

- First, it is brought about by Christ himself. When he is held up, he draws all men to himself, which happens each time the gospel is proclaimed. I did not say preached, although preaching is normally necessary, for Jesus is proclaimed in many other ways besides preaching.

- Secondly, this great offer by God is not just for Jews or any particular group of people, but for the whole world; no one is excluded. The conservative Calvinists of the sixteenth century (and later some groups of Baptists) were so concerned to make salvation a free gift independent of merit that they concluded that even the response to the gospel was entirely a gift and not given to all. Jacob Arminius, a theology professor at the University of Leiden, challenged those brands of Calvinism that seemed to condemn people who had no choice in the matter, but were lost by the absolute election of God. The controversy became savage, though Arminius himself remained peaceable throughout. He was not tried for heresy but allowed to defend his positions in a statement before the assembly of the states in Holland. John 3:16 was a most important verse for Arminius and "whosoever" the most important word in it. One of the English observers at the Dutch debate remarked that when he heard Arminius expound John 3:16, he bade John Calvin goodnight. The English church generally followed Arminius. There remained, however, a Calvinist wing of the evangelical movement, but the Methodist wing of the movement was strongly pro-Arminian, as were John and Charles Wesley. Largely due to John Wesley's influence, American Protestantism became largely Arminian with many Presbyterians following suit. Modern Calvinists, indeed, tend to the view that the strict form of Calvinism does not really represent the views of the great John Calvin, who held that predestination and free will were both taught in the scriptures and that the relation between them was a mystery known to God but not fully by us. Luther definitely took this position, saying that predestination existed only in the mind of God and that we mortals should go with free will.

The Woman at the Well

John 4:1-42

Now Jesus learned that the Pharisees had heard that he was gaining and baptizing more disciples than John—although in fact it was not Jesus who baptized, but his disciples. So he left Judea and went back once more to Galilee.

Now he had to go through Samaria. So he came to a town in Samaria called Sychar, near the plot of ground Jacob had given to his son Joseph. Jacob's well was there, and Jesus, tired as he was from the journey, sat down by the well. It was about noon.

When a Samaritan woman came to draw water, Jesus said to her, "Will you give me a drink?" (His disciples had gone into the town to buy food.) (vv. 1-8)

Read through verse 42 in your Bible.

Comment

1 This is one of several stories in John's Gospel that describes how Jesus actually talked with individuals. John was not actually present on these occasions, certainly not on this one, but he must have pieced the story together from what others told him or even from what he learned from Jesus himself. He was, after all, the beloved disciple.

2 It is somewhat odd that Jesus and his disciples traveled through Samaria. Relations between the two communities were so bad that Jews traveling between Galilee and Judea normally went the long way around, crossing and recrossing the Jordan and so avoiding Samaria. Jesus may indeed have deliberately gone directly through Samaria in order to have this interview, breaking through the curtain of hatred between the two communities in order that the Samaritans might get to meet their Messiah. It would be typical of Jesus if this were so, for he told the parable of the good Samaritan and noted that the only cleansed leper who returned to him to give thanks for his healing was a Samaritan.

3 It was an odd time for the woman to come and draw water—noon, the hottest period in the day. But this woman had a bad reputation: she had married man after man and did not care to be exposed to the barbs and jests of the other women drawing water.

4 When she met Jesus, she was astounded by two things: first, that a Jewish man would speak to an unaccompanied woman; second, that he would speak to a Samaritan. This story shows the great kindliness and thoughtfulness of Jesus when dealing with people, especially people who were normally treated as trash. He opens the conversation by asking for a drink of water, an unthreatening gambit. She expressed surprise that he would ask for water from a woman and a Samaritan woman at that. Jesus then offers her "living water," which literally is water flowing in a stream, not still as in a pond. She takes this literally and asks him how he expects to give her this living water. Jesus leads her on further by explaining that the water he was talking about was not ordinary water, but such that if you tasted it, you would never thirst again. She asks him how on earth he can supply such water. She was probably aware at this stage in the conversation that he was reaching into the deeper waters of her heart and life. Jesus then goes straight to her real need, her disordered life. He asks her to call her husband. She now knows what he is really talking about and moves defensively. She sidesteps into a theological controversy, the proper site for a center of worship. Jesus steers the conversation back to the real issue: it does not matter where you worship but how you worship. She tries another theoretical sidestep, saying essentially that we are getting into deep questions here that will only be answered when the Messiah comes. Jesus then informs here that she is speaking to the Messiah, and she believes him.

5 The rest of this story is about the outcome of this conversation. The woman brought a crowd of her townsfolk to see Jesus, saying, "This man told me everything I ever did. Is not this the Messiah?" And after Jesus had delayed two more days and talked with them some more, they too believed, saying, "Now we believe not just because you told us, for we have seen with our eyes and know that this is the Christ, the chosen one of God." Jesus had created a new body of disciples in this unlikely place.

6 This is a great missionary story, of course, but it also mirrors the way in which Jesus deals with each one of us as individuals. It is like a conversation. He gently approaches us and reveals to us our need, then meets all our evasions and excuses until we are ready to accept him, and finally sends us to spread abroad what we have received.

The Transfiguration

Matthew 17:1-9

After six days Jesus took with him Peter, James and John the brother of James, and led them up a high mountain by themselves. There he was transfigured before them. His face shone like the sun, and his clothes became as white as the light. Just then there appeared before them Moses and Elijah, talking with Jesus.

Peter said to Jesus, "Lord, it is good for us to be here. If you wish, I will put up three shelters—one for you, one for Moses and one for Elijah."

While he was still speaking, a bright cloud covered them, and a voice from the cloud said, "This is my Son, whom I love; with him I am well pleased. Listen to him!"

When the disciples heard this, they fell facedown to the ground, terrified. But Jesus came and touched them. "Get up," he said. "Don't be afraid." When they looked up, they saw no one except Jesus.

As they were coming down the mountain, Jesus instructed them, "Don't tell anyone what you have seen, until the Son of Man has been raised from the dead."

Comment

1 This event closely follows Peter's confession at Caesarea Philippi that Jesus was the Christ, the Son of the Living God. The disciples—or at least the inner core of Peter, James, and John, the advanced pupils—were to receive a remarkable confirmation of that confession, no doubt necessary as they were about to be sorely tested by the crucifixion of their Lord and master and commissioned to take the gospel message beyond Judaism to the whole world.

2 They saw Jesus in his glory, the reality behind the earthly figure, represented as the consummation of the biblical revelation of God, with Moses representing the Law and Elijah the prophets, the two together roughly representing the sum of the biblical revelation of the Old Testament.

3 The voice from heaven then commanded him, saying, "This is my Son, the beloved; listen to him."

4 This event places Jesus where he belongs, right in the center of the Bible. We interpret what went before as the long lead-up to the coming of Jesus, and what follows in the Gospels we view and understand as presenting Jesus and what he did and said. The Acts and the Epistles describe the foundation of his body, the church, and the Apocalypse describes the triumph of the Lamb.

5 This event also tells us what we are expected to do as disciples of Jesus: listen to, follow, and live by him. As St. Paul said, "The life I now live in the body, I live by faith in the Son of God, who loved me and gave himself for me" (Gal 2:20). We may not do so perfectly, but we must do so, like King David of old, with our whole heart. That is what being a Christian means.

The Lord's Prayer

Matthew 6:9-13

"This, then, is how you should pray:
'Our Father in heaven,
hallowed be your name,
your kingdom come,
your will be done,
on earth as it is in heaven.
Give us today our daily bread.
And forgive us our debts,
as we also have forgiven our debtors.
And lead us not into temptation,
but deliver us from the evil one.'"

See also Matthew 6 and Luke 11.

Comment

1 It is important to note the place of prayer in Jesus' life. In his busy life, often early in the morning when he had peace and quiet, he would slip away and commune with his Father in heaven. His contact must have been intimate and direct, for he said he taught nothing but what he had heard from his Father and accomplished most of the things that he did by requesting them from God and by the power of God. He said, for instance, that he cast out demons by the finger of God, and the raising of Lazarus from the dead was in response to a prayer from Jesus.

2 No wonder the disciples asked Jesus to teach them to pray. His prayers showed them they had a lot to learn. Jesus responded with his model prayer. It is not a full and complete prayer but rather a model, a short outline of what prayer is about, a set of headings describing the essence of praying.

3 *Our Father in heaven, your name be holy.* The first part has to do with entering into God's presence, and especially remembering who he is, our Father in heaven. So we begin with worship. The term *worship* is a foreshortening of the Anglo-Saxon word *worth-ship*, which was used annually when the notables of the realm came to offer their loyalty to their sovereign Lord the king. In this act they

expressed their heartfelt sense of who and how important the Sovereign was. They thereupon pledged their loyalty and obedience as was appropriate to such a one. And this is how we begin to pray: remembering what God has revealed of himself in the awesome wonders of the universe and how he has shown us who he is in the incarnation. Ignatius Loyola taught his initiates to use their imagination as they prayed—to think on the vastness of the universe and also that they were actually in the presence of Jesus and about to hold a conversation with him. This is how we should begin prayer, with a spell of meditation so that God and his Son are not just words to us but real persons we are talking *with* (I did not say talking *to*).

4 *Hallowed be thy name.* The name of God, given to Moses was EHWH (meaning "I Am"). When Moses passed this name on to the Israelites, it became JHWH ("He is"). It is thought that because of the great reverence in which the Israelites held God's name, they rarely took it on their lips at all and mostly used the alternative ADONAI ("the Lord"), as we commonly do today. So when the Masoretic scholars wrote the name of God JHWH, they added the vowels of ADONAI, which was much later taken to mean "Jehovah." This reverence for the name of a loved one is part of our own makeup. We would be upset if someone started casually using the name of our mother or father in a coarse joke, for example. Likewise, we should make it known, by our obvious attitude without necessarily saying a word, that the casual use of the name of God or Christ or Jesus as an expletive is offensive to us.

5 *May your kingdom come and your will be done on earth as it is in heaven.* We live in a world where two processes are going on at the same time—one quiet, the other assertive and noisy. The quiet one is God's kingdom growing and proceeding silently, as it must, so that we often feel as if nothing is happening. The other is loud and vociferous, proclaiming with brass trumpets and great lambeg drums the progress and expected triumphs of God's enemies. Some of these are evil empires; others are associations of influential people who work for and loudly predict the end of the Christian faith and the church. But as we pray the Lord's Prayer, we remember that God's servants are also busy and that the almighty creator and controller of the universe is behind them and with them, that his rule is proceeding and the end is assured. This is the message of the Apocalypse. Hallelujah, for the Lord God omnipotent reigneth.

6 *Give us day by day our daily bread.* We forget in our stable and generally prosperous society that in ancient times, and in large parts of the world today, bread on the table was by no means guaranteed. But we have other needs and

serious concerns for our daily living, and we hold these up before our heavenly Father, assured of his concern for our needs. His answers are seldom spectacular—a parachute with a large check attached does not arrive from heaven—but quietly and secretly he is working on our behalf. A favorite saying of my mother was "Between having and wanting, we will get what will do us."

7 *Forgive us our sins as we forgive those who sin against us.* Jesus has told us that all of our sins can be forgiven except one, the sin against the Holy Spirit. This is when we hear the call of Jesus and turn away, preferring to stick to our own way. The Pharisees saw the miracles and heard Jesus' words but still killed him to protect their own position in the nation. A dying man once said to me, "I have lived without God, and I will die without God," an awful way to go into eternity. But forgiveness is conditional. Jesus told a story of man who was forgiven a vast sum and then took a fellow servant by the throat who owed him a paltry amount. His forgiveness was thereupon revoked.

8 *Lead us not into a time of trial, but deliver us from the evil one.* This is often mistranslated as "lead us not into temptation," for James the Lord's brother has told us plainly that God is not tempted, nor does he tempt anyone (Jas 1). Jesus is referring here to times of trial, whether persecution or some other disaster. We are not required to put our necks into the noose. Quite the contrary, if we are persecuted in one city, we are advised to flee to another one. We have two great examples to follow here: Job, who held on to God in the midst of his suffering; and Shadrach, Meshach, and Abednego, who, threatened with the fiery furnace of King Nebuchadnezzar if they did not worship the golden idol, replied, "If we are thrown into the blazing furnace, the God we serve is able to deliver us from it, and he will deliver us from Your Majesty's hand. But even if he does not, we want you to know, Your Majesty, that we will not serve your gods or worship the image of gold you have set up" (Dan 3:17-18).

9 *For thine is the kingdom and the power and the glory forever. Amen.* This is how we should rise from our knees after praying this prayer from our hearts: triumphant and assured, all worries gone, ready for anything that will come.

10 It is notable that there are no prayers for other people or causes in this prayer. It is entirely personal. But as we read elsewhere in Jesus' teachings, we will find other kinds of prayer. Jesus prayed for all sorts of things, including Lazarus's resurrection from the dead We are told to ask and we will receive, seek and we will find, knock and it shall be opened to us. St. Paul also urges us to pray for all sorts and conditions of mankind.

The Widow's Mite

Luke 21:1-4

As Jesus looked up, he saw the rich putting their gifts into the temple treasury. He also saw a poor widow put in two very small copper coins. "Truly I tell you," he said, "this poor widow has put in more than all the others. All these people gave their gifts out of their wealth; but she out of her poverty put in all she had to live on."

Comment

1 A *lepton* (translated "mite" in the KJV) was the tiniest coin in the Greek world. Various equivalents have been calculated for the two lepta, which would have been a tiny gift, about as little as you could give (next to nothing in absolute terms). But it was all the poor widow had. As a Jewish widow, she would receive a donation of food twice a week and perhaps a little money.

2 This poor woman, with nobody to support her and cash very scarce, had managed to accumulate a couple lepta. But when she went up to the temple to pray, from the fullness of her heart she gave them to God. They were not much, but they were all that she had.

3 Jesus, who was watching this happen, commented that hers was the greatest contribution of all, for he was using a different measure of a gift, considering it as a fraction of the giver's total wealth. A gift of a dollar would be nothing to a person of enormous wealth, but a great deal to someone living on Social Security. I once gave a small amount to missions or some such and told my mother about it, expecting praise. But her comment (based on this story) was, "How much did you keep?"

4 The point of the story is generosity toward God's work in response to God's generosity to each of us. We need to gladly support the church, which is Christ's body. We are also surrounded, even at home, by people who are poor, and the situation all over the world is much worse with people actually dying of starvation and disease. God's people everywhere need our support, financial and otherwise.

5 John Wesley believed that giving was the surest sign of Christian devotion. He was concerned that the Methodist people had become more wealthy by their honesty and industry and that they were not giving generously enough. He declared that if he died and owned more than ten pounds, he would count himself a robber. He received considerable amounts of money during his lifetime by his writings and other means, but his estate when he died consisted of a set of silver spoons worth exactly ten pounds. In his famous sermon on the use of money, he offered the following advice: Make all you can, save all you can, and give all you can. There is no more satisfying use of money than to give it away to someone who needs it.

The Triumphal Entry into Jerusalem

Luke 19:29-40

As he approached Beth-phage and Bethany at the hill called the Mount of Ol-ives, he sent two of his dis-ciples, saying to them, "Go to the village ahead of you, and as you enter it, you will find a colt tied there, which no one has ever ridden. Un-tie it and bring it here. If anyone asks you, 'Why are you untying it?' say, 'The Lord needs it.'" (vv. 29-31)

Read through verse 40 in your Bible.

Comment

1 This great event is celebrat-ed in our churches on Palm Sunday when the children parade in waving palm leaves and crying, "Hosanna to the Son of David." But why was this event so important? It was one more example of the acted parables that the prophets and others used to make a statement in a telling manner. Jesus was proclaiming in this graphic way that he was the Messiah who had come to save his people as the prophets had foretold. Jesus had revealed himself to his disciples at the transfiguration; he is now revealing himself to the nation and to us.

2 Two groups that were there witnessing this event didn't get the message. The ordinary onlookers, including the disciples, thought that Jesus, as Messiah, was going to drive out the Romans and establish the kingdom of Israel as it had been in the time of King David. The Pharisees and rulers, on the other hand, were appalled that Jesus, or any other ordinary human being, should claim to be the

Messiah, and they called on Jesus to tell his disciples to be quiet. But Jesus knew he was acting on the orders of his heavenly Father and told them that if his disciples were quiet, the very stones would cry out.

3 This is typical of the way God acts. If he spoke and acted openly, everyone would get in line and behave, but they would not be the creatures God has made in his image, obeying him and enjoying him freely; they would be automatons, mere robots. So God makes himself and his message plain to those who have the eyes to see and the heart to respond, as here, where Jesus is being clearly presented as the messianic king. But he does not force himself on the unwilling and self-willed and rebellious. They will be blind and deaf to the message, and still are.

The Crucifixion

Matthew 27

As they were going out, they met a man from Cyrene, named Simon, and they forced him to carry the cross. They came to a place called Golgotha (which means "the place of the skull"). There they offered Jesus wine to drink, mixed with gall; but after tasting it, he refused to drink it. When they had crucified him, they divided up his clothes by casting lots. And sitting down, they kept watch over him there. Above his head they placed the written charge against him: THIS IS JESUS, THE KING OF THE JEWS. (vv. 32-27)

Read through verse 54 in your Bible.

Comment

1 The crucifixion story is not uniform in all the Gospels. The writers described the events as they had seen them or heard of them. Each selected different items, which they put together as they saw fit. This is all the more convincing as to the truth of their story just as the truth about a road accident can be better pieced together from the reports of several bystanders. Indeed, it is difficult to see how they could or would have concocted this story, in view of the fact that this was not done in a corner and could easily have been contradicted by other witnesses. The principal objection would be that the story is so unlike our ordinary experience that it is unbelievable. But this was no ordinary occurrence. We would expect the event to be marked by miraculous interpretative events.

2 One Gospel says that Christ, before he was crucified, was offered wine mixed with *gall*, another that it was mixed with myrrh. The term gall means a bitter-tasting substance and was commonly used to refer to poison. Jesus, after tasting it, refused it, either because he thought it was poison (unlikely) or because he thought it was offered as an analgesic and he had chosen to suffer crucifixion to the full. The other term used is *myrrh* (which was offered as a gift to Jesus by the wise men), which also means bitter. Myrrh is a resin obtained from small bushes and is used in perfumes and also in medicine. It would have the same significance as gall to Jesus, since myrrh was an analgesic operating on the same receptors as opiates.

3 The savagery and cruelty of the crucifixion is clearly seen in the gospel story. The victims were first stripped, then whipped with the dreadful Roman flagellum to within an inch of their lives. The flagellum had several cords, as many as five, which had little jagged pieces of metal inserted into the thongs so that they cut deep into the flesh, laying bare the bones of the rib cage. One purpose of this was to weaken the prisoner by pain and blood loss so that they would not last too long when they were crucified. Care was taken to avoid whipping over the area of the kidneys as this might cause them to expire too soon. Pain and death were produced by hanging them up so that gravity would cause the blood to pool down into the legs and lower part of the body. This produced extreme ischemic pain, which the victim could alleviate by pushing themselves up with their legs, pumping the blood back toward the heart. This helped for a little while, after which time they tired and sagged down again and the torture proceeded all over again, until they were too weak to push and died. This could take days, and if they wanted to hurry the process up, as they did in Jesus' crucifixion when the Sabbath approached, the soldiers would break the victim's legs so they could not push with them. They did this to the two robbers crucified along with Jesus, but when they came to Jesus, he was already dead.

4 The miracles that surrounded Jesus' death are powerful interpreting tools, "signs" as John's Gospel calls them. The darkness over the land represents the omnipresent power of evil covering the earth. The tearing apart of the great veil separating the holy of holies from the rest of the temple signifies the opening of the way into the presence of God for all who receive the Messiah. The raising of many saints from the dead and their strolling around Jerusalem demonstrates the gift of eternal life for all who believe in him. The sayings of Jesus on the cross have the same significance. Jesus' cry, "My God, why have you forsaken me?" reveals the barring of Jesus from his Father's presence as he took upon himself the sin of the whole world. His cry "finished" is a shout of triumph with the completion of the sacrificial offering of himself for our sins.

5 All this is clear enough and understandable, but the ultimate nature of the event is a mystery—something to be grasped by faith but somewhat beyond our powers of imagining. Most, if not all, of the explanations of the sacrifice of Christ put forward by the great minds of the past (and for that matter the present) fall short and fail to make it clear to us how the sufferings and death of one person can accrue to the benefit of the rest of us. But it is very clear what the Bible is saying to us on the subject, namely that the sufferings and death of Jesus were a

sacrifice for our sins, by which salvation becomes available to all mankind. It is a mystery, but we do not need to be afraid of mysteries. Not only the Bible but science and life itself are full of mysteries. This is not to say there is no explanation of them, but in our present state of knowledge, even extending into the imaginable future, there is no rational explanation of them. The best we can say about them is, as Descartes had to say about the great mystery of vision (how light flowing through the eye into the mind produces the solid world of common experience), is that God knows.

6 The most important question about the atonement is how we appropriate its benefits for ourselves. The answer of the New Testament is clear: If we confess with our mouths the Lord Jesus and believe in our hearts that God raised him from the dead, we shall be saved (Rom 10:9). Both items are necessary—confession with the mouth (no secret disciples) and believing in the heart (the very center of our being). He is still seeking us, knocking at the door of our hearts (Rev 3:20), and if we let him in, it is party time.

The Seven Utterances of Jesus on the Cross

1. "Father, forgive them, for they do not know what they are doing."
   Luke 23:34

2. "Truly I tell you, today you will be with me in paradise."
   Luke 23:43

3. "Woman, here is your son"; "Here is your mother."
   John 19:26, 27

4. My God, my God, why have you forsaken me?"
   Matthew 27:46; Mark 15:34

5. "I am thirsty."
   John 19:28

6. "It is finished."
   John 19:30

7. "Father, into your hands I commit my spirit."
   Luke 23:46

Comment

1 These seven sayings, together with the miracles that accompanied the crucifixion, provide the best interpretation and comment that we could imagine of this mighty salvation event. The sayings are spread over all four Gospels, only one of them in more than one Gospel, and their order and even the texts differ here and there. But this is what we should expect, for nowhere in the Bible (outside the Ten Commandments in Exod 20) did God present us with an authorized version written on rock with a laser, but allowed the authors to describe them as and how they saw or heard them. One might have preferred that God should write a single account in his own words, but in his wisdom he chose to rely on the memories of the authors. And this was indeed wise, for coming from several witnesses in slightly different wordings, the result is more convincing and also allows a better understanding of the events described.

2 The accompanying miracles make it clear that this was no ordinary death, but a mighty event, opening the gates of heaven to all who would believe in the Savior. So there was darkness over the land from the sixth to the ninth hour, representing evil overshadowing the earth. Then at the ninth hour the veil of the

temple was torn in two from top to bottom. This was a huge, thick curtain separating the outer courts, where people and priests could enter freely, from the innermost chamber, where the ark of the covenant rested, representing God's presence. Only the high priest could enter here and only once a year when the great sacrifice for sin was offered. This event represented the beginning of a new era, opening the way into God's presence to all who would believe in God's Son and receive the benefits of his sacrifice for their sins.

3 The first saying, "Father, forgive them," has been a model for Christian martyrs ever since. And it is appropriate, for angry mobs seldom know what they are doing and therefore need some forgiving. It was quite another matter with the highly placed Jews who spoke with Jesus and saw the miracles of his ministry but sought his life because he was threatening their position. This carries guilt, and all we can do is commend them to the mercy of God, who knows the hearts of men and who alone can judge. And we must also love these enemies too and pray for them.

4 The promise to the dying thief has been a beacon of hope to people who have gone so far down the wrong path that they despair of ever finding their way back. The wonderful message of this saying is that it is never too late to seek the mercy of God and attain salvation. St. Augustine's comment was that there were two thieves: one to tell us never to despair and the other to warn us not to presume that all will somehow be well with us. But although deathbed repentance and salvation is available and should certainly be sought, it is hardly advisable to leave such an important matter so late. When he was dying, my father told my mother he was glad he had found salvation earlier, for he was too busy dying now to attend to it. An old Scottish elder was dying, and his minister wanted him to commend his soul to God. But he said, "I thatched my house in good weather; the storm's up now."

5 In his agony—and crucifixion was prolonged and continuous agony—Jesus did not forget his mother and made provision for her, leaving her in the care of the beloved disciple. This was necessary as she would certainly no longer have been considered eligible for the Jewish provisions for the poor and needy. She had suffered much, but Jesus knew and understood how she was feeling and even in his agony remembered to provide for her.

6 Jesus called out that he was thirsty. This was not just the ordinary thirst that we experience when we need a drink of water; it was the dreadful thirst of cardiovascular shock. Crucifixion causes blood to pool in the lower body and results in a dreadful thirst. The soldiers offered him sour wine on a sponge with a narcotic pain-relieving drug in it. And this he refused, for he knew that it was his destiny to suffer, not to avoid suffering. He was going to drink that cup to the full.

7 One of the most difficult sayings on the cross is the only one spoken in his native language, Aramaic: "My God, my God, why have you forsaken me?" This was not because he thought that God had let him down. Rather, he was bearing the ultimate penalty of sin, separation from God. This must have been a dreadful experience for one who had been at one with his Father all the time. Jesus' agony in the garden was not just fear of death, for he had told his disciples not to fear those who could only kill the body but could not touch the soul. It was something much more profound, related to his bearing the sin of the world. He had to drink the cup prepared for him and continue in his obedience to the Father.

8 But the last word, "It is finished," is not a word of defeat but of triumph. We do not know what the Aramaic words were, but the Greek is in the pluperfect tense, "It is now completed," and was followed by the last saying, an expression of complete faith and trust: "Father, into thy hands I commend my spirit."

9 These comments do not profess to explain the mystery of Christ's sacrifice on the cross. Different terms are used in the Bible, and different explanations have been offered by great theologians since. But like many other things in the Bible, and indeed outside it, it remains unimaginable, a mystery. But it is firmly embedded in the Bible. Dr. Vincent Taylor, a mighty New Testament scholar and theologian, wrote two books about the atonement, both showing how deeply ingrained this idea of a necessary sacrificial death for the forgiveness of sins was: *Jesus and His Sacrifice* and *The Atonement in New Testament Teaching*. We cannot fully understand it, but we can appreciate it as a loving sacrificial act of God in Christ on our behalf.

The Resurrection

John 20

Early on the first day of the week, while it was still dark, Mary Magdalene went to the tomb and saw that the stone had been removed from the entrance. So she came running to Simon Peter and the other disciple, the one Jesus loved, and said, "They have taken the Lord out of the tomb, and we don't know where they have put him!" (vv. 1-2)

Read though verse 29 in your Bible.

Comment

1 When the women who had gone to the tomb to embalm Jesus' body returned and told the assembled disciples that they had seen the Lord, their words seemed to them as idle tales. But this was a special event, following a special life and a special death, and needs to be looked at a little more closely. When the

women found the empty tomb, an angel (or two angels) told them, "He is not here. He is risen." They ran and told the disciples what they had seen and heard. Though skeptical, Peter and John ran to the tomb and looked in and saw the linen cloths lying. They must have been in the original wrapped condition but with no body inside. John, the beloved disciple who went into the cave and saw the linen clothes lying and the face cloth over by itself, thereupon believed. Jesus himself appeared to Mary Magdalene. As a woman, she would not be allowed to testify in a Jewish court, but we have no such prejudice. Afterward, Jesus appeared to the disciples, who were hiding in the upper room for fear of the Jews, and later to the two walking from Jerusalem to Emmaus. Then he met them on the shore of the lake when they had gone back to their old jobs as fishermen. What had these men to gain from making up a tale? Most of them from then on had a hard life and a violent death for their reward. If we are reasoning horizontally, comparing different possibilities side by side, the idea of the resurrection is much more convincing than any of the alternatives. Especially, we must remember who we are talking about. Jesus is the Messiah. I would expect it of him.

2 We consider now the evidence of the Shroud of Turin, the strange image, front and back views, of a crucified man who had been scourged. If you want to hear nonsense, listen to its critics. The carbon dating, which put the shroud in the mid-thirteenth century, is treated as a scientific fact, exposing the fraud. One critic even claimed that the dating of the shroud by the carbon dating must be correct because three separate labs got the same result (ignoring the fact that they examined three fragments from the same sample). Another critic painted a corpse with some sticky material and got a negative image and concluded that they had shown how the image on the shroud might have been produced. The carbon dating is now generally acknowledged to have been grossly mishandled. The sample was taken, and not properly cleaned, from a part of the shroud that had been rewoven following damage in a thirteenth-century fire. But let us now look at the evidence from the shroud itself.

3 The image itself is peculiar. It was studied intensively by a group of heavyweight scientists from the space center in Nassau, many of whom had expected to see a fake and quite a number of whom later concluded that it was indeed the burial shroud of Jesus for the following reasons:

a. It is a negative image, and it is not a painting. There is no pigment, other than some daubs put on by artists working on it. In fact, the image is entirely superficial, with no penetration into the linen material.

This kind of surface marking is typical of a nuclear radiation effect, which is currently producible but would have been virtually impossible to manage in the thirteenth century.

b. It is also strange in that the shroud image can be used to make a hologram, a three-dimensional image, which is found in images produced by radiation but cannot be carried out with a single photographic image or a painting.

c. Certain features of the image show a knowledge of crucifixion unknown to later artists, especially in the thirteenth century. The nail prints are conventionally placed by artists in the center of the palm, which would be ridiculous as the weight of the body would tear them through the flesh and out between the fingers. The shroud nail prints are where they should be, in the carpal bones just proximal to the palm of the hand.

d. The blood on the shroud is real blood of the same ABA pattern as that found on the sudarion, the face cloth, which is preserved in Oviedo in Spain. The face cloth has no image for obvious reasons, but a forger might well have put an image there too.

e. Less decisive but interesting are the marks of the flogging Jesus received. This was done by two soldiers, one standing on either side and striking alternately, producing the crisscross pattern seen on the back of the figure. The blows also avoid the region of the kidneys, an important point as the Romans wished to avoid internal damage that would kill the victim too quickly.

f. Close examination of the shroud revealed pollen embedded in the material, which was removed on adhesive tape and examined under the microscope. The presence of pollen is not surprising since it was the Jewish custom to put flowers in the winding sheet. What is interesting about the pollen in the shroud is that much of it comes from flowers that bloom in the region of Jerusalem about the right time of year and not elsewhere. So the forger would have to have journeyed to Jerusalem, collected the appropriate pollen, and then dusted it into the sheet.

g. High-resolution photographic plates of the shroud were made in the late nineteenth century and have been used by shroud researchers ever since. Images of a number of artifacts can be seen, which careful examination shows to be flowers, nails, and what appears to be a part of a notice board with lettering on it. The flowers are interesting since they are the same flowers as shown by the pollen. Even more interesting is the image of a thorny plant, which may have been the original crown of thorns. Avinoam Danin, a botanist with the Hebrew University in Jerusalem, has identified this image with a thorny plant growing in the vicinity of Jerusalem. He is not a Christian but is convinced that the evidence points to the shroud being the burial cloth of Jesus. The board is a fragment with some letters discernable on it, consistent with the inscription described in Mark's Gospel. There is even the image of a coin (that would be placed on the eyes by Joseph of Arimathea), identified as one extant in the first century. The nails are large and crude, such as were used by Roman army engineers. All these things would be included in the winding sheet because they would have the victim's blood on them and so, according to the Jewish way of thinking, they were part of the body.

h. What should we conclude from this? Dr. Alan Whanger, a psychiatrist and photographic expert, now retired from Duke University Hospital, who first introduced me to the shroud, while he is convinced that it is genuine, expresses himself in very cautious scientific terms that the evidence is consistent with it being the winding cloth of Jesus. I myself, as a horizontal logician, would pronounce on the basis of this evidence that the view that the shroud is genuine is a clear winner.

The Ascension of Jesus into Heaven

Acts 1:1-11

In my former book, Theophilus, I wrote about all that Jesus began to do and to teach until the day he was taken up to heaven, after giving instructions through the Holy Spirit to the apostles he had chosen. After his suffering, he presented himself to them and gave many convincing proofs that he was alive. He appeared to them over a period of forty days and spoke about the kingdom of God. On one occasion, while he was eating with them, he gave them this command: "Do not leave Jerusalem, but wait for the gift my Father promised, which you have heard me speak about. For John baptized with water, but in a few days you will be baptized with the Holy Spirit."

Then they gathered around him and asked him, "Lord, are you at this time going to restore the kingdom to Israel?"

He said to them: "It is not for you to know the times or dates the Father has set by his own authority. But you will receive power when the Holy Spirit comes on you; and you will be my witnesses in Jerusalem, and in all Judea and Samaria, and to the ends of the earth."

After he said this, he was taken up before their very eyes, and a cloud hid him from their sight.

They were looking intently up into the sky as he was going, when suddenly two men dressed in white stood beside them. "Men of Galilee," they said, "why do you stand here looking into the sky? This same Jesus, who has been taken from you into heaven, will come back in the same way you have seen him go into heaven."

Comment

1 The description of this event seems odd to us since our picture of the universe is decidedly different to that of the first disciples, who described the world the way they saw it, like a bowl hanging over the plate of the earth with water all around, sprinkling down and surging up and generally surrounding the land. So why did Jesus leave the disciples in this rather odd manner? I think it was because after forty days, seeing him again and again, there had to be a definite signing off event in terms that the disciples would understand.

2 They also had definite instructions as to what they were to do: return to Jerusalem and wait for the next event, the coming of the Holy Spirit.

3 In answer to their continuing misunderstanding of the kingdom of God, they were told that it was none of their business, and their attention was drawn to the wider promise of the kingdom: it was to be for the whole world, not just the Jews.

4 Finally, they were told that Jesus would return in glory, the second advent at the end of the age, the great event to which we all look forward with anticipation.

5 The acclamation in the Communion service tells us the essence of our continuing faith: "Christ has died, Christ has risen, Christ will come again."

My Yoke Is Easy, and My Burden Is Light

Matthew 11:28-30

"Come to me, all you who are weary and burdened, and I will give you rest. Take my yoke upon you and learn from me, for I am gentle and humble in heart, and you will find rest for your souls. For my yoke is easy and my burden is light."

Comment

1 Jesus was a carpenter; as such, he would have built or constructed many things that we no longer use today, having substituted tractors and other mechanical devices for draft animals and farming in general. He would certainly have made yokes. Plato said that a thoughtful person, other things being equal, would make better shoes or anything else, and we cannot imagine Jesus making yokes that didn't fit well or were roughly finished or that in any other way might irritate or injure the animal. His yokes would fit well and be smooth. Also, being considerate, he would not work an animal to death by overloading it or making it work too long without a rest.

2 Farmers in America and Canada and in third-world countries still use yokes and draft animals. There is indeed a move to revive the use of draft animals in smaller farms. They are, of course, still much in use in competitions.

3 There are three main types of yoke, the neck yoke being the most common, but head yokes and withers yokes are still used in various parts of the world. It is important, especially with the neck yoke, to have the yoke fitted well to the neck of the animal to avoid discomfort and also galls and sores. Indeed, the care of the animal is a major consideration in the use of yokes generally.

4 Jesus applied these considerations to his other and greater work: gathering the children of God into his kingdom and under his care. God uses human intermediaries to do his work in the world; we are God's coworkers. He provides the main conditions, but we are responsible for putting them to work in God's world. The tasks of spreading the good news, of running his church, of feeding the hungry, helping the distressed, and many more things require the cooperation of his human helpers.

5 But like a good cattle drover, he looks after his helpers. He will not ask us to do more than we can bear and will take care that we are not burned out in the process. Indeed, he is with us, working alongside us, encouraging and cheering and comforting us as we pull together.

6 Comforters were not people who patted the warriors on the head and said, "There, there." They carried their weapons, fought alongside the warriors, and generally helped them in battle, which is how God works with us. Remember how God sustained and comforted Elijah when he was on the run from Jezebel and fearing for his life.

7 There is an old story about a traveler who had noticed a set of footsteps beside his own in the sand, and so far as he was aware, there was nobody there. So he asked God what they meant, and God said, "That was when I walked beside you." But after a while the footprints disappeared, and he asked God what that meant. God replied, "That was when I carried you."

The Good Shepherd and the Lost Sheep

Luke 15:1-7

Now the tax collectors and sinners were all gathering around to hear Jesus. But the Pharisees and the teachers of the law muttered, "This man welcomes sinners and eats with them."

Then Jesus told them this parable: "Suppose one of you has a hundred sheep and loses one of them. Doesn't he leave the ninety-nine in the open country and go after the lost sheep until he finds it? And when he finds it, he joyfully puts it on his shoulders and goes home. Then he calls his friends and neighbors together and says, 'Rejoice with me; I have found my lost sheep.' I tell you that in the same way there will be more rejoicing in heaven over one sinner who repents than over ninety-nine righteous persons who do not need to repent."

See also Matthew 18:12-14.

Comment

1 The context of this parable is that the scribes and Pharisees, orthodox Jews, were grumbling about Jesus keeping company and eating with sinners like Zacchaeus the tax collector, prostitutes, and lost souls generally. So Jesus told them this parable about a good shepherd and a lost sheep.

2 A lost sheep was nothing unusual in those days when there were no fences and generally open grazing. Sheep are notorious for following a food source and getting hopelessly lost. And there is nothing new in people doing the same thing. Many of these lost souls might well agree with the Pharisees that they are beyond hope. "We have made our bed," they may say," so we must lie on it." Such people tend to stay aloof from the church and God and simply carry on down the broad way that has no future.

3 The way of the world is to despise them and leave them to their fate. But Jesus is telling us that God's attitude is different. He is grieved and mourns for them just like a good parent with a wayward child. And the story is not about us repenting and trying to find our way back to God. God in Christ is actively seeking us.

4 There is a story about an extremely stern and strict Presbyterian elder, a widower, whose only daughter was sweet-talked into running away with some

rascal of a man. Her father went to the presbytery and demanded that her name be struck off the church roll. Wisely, they refused and prayed for her return. The father became sterner than ever, but later he began to mourn for her instead of harshly blaming her. The daughter was eventually abandoned by her plausible seducer and in despair found her way one evening into a Methodist church (I like this story). They were singing a hymn (abomination to her father), and she opened her heart and her misery to the Good Shepherd. One evening shortly thereafter, she came back home and nervously tapped on the door. When her father opened the door and saw her, his heart melted, and he took her in his arms and used all the dozen or so Gaelic words for "darling." His whole character was changed, and his stern theology was made over accordingly in a much warmer mold. He even started singing hymns.

5 One of Jesus' makeovers to the Law of Moses is relevant here. Jesus said, "You have heard that it was said, 'Love your neighbor and hate your enemy.' But I tell you, love your enemies and pray for those who persecute you, that you may be children of your Father in heaven. He causes his sun to rise on the evil and the good, and sends rain on the righteous and the unrighteous" (Matt 5:43-45).

6 Jesus is not supporting pacifist politics. We have the right and indeed the duty to resist evil, as when the Nazis were exterminating Jews and radical Islamists are massacring any who are not Muslim. But we must at the same time feel for them and pray that they may come to a better frame of mind. We might even pray the prayer of Jesus on the cross: "Father, forgive them, for they know not what they do."

The Parable of the Crooked Judge

Luke 18:1-8

Then Jesus told his disciples a parable to show them that they should always pray and not give up. He said: "In a certain town there was a judge who neither feared God nor cared what people thought. And there was a widow in that town who kept coming to him with the plea, 'Grant me justice against my adversary.'

"For some time he refused. But finally he said to himself, 'Even though I don't fear God or care what people think, yet because this widow keeps bothering me, I will see that she gets justice, so that she won't eventually come and attack me!'"

And the Lord said, "Listen to what the unjust judge says. And will not God bring about justice for his chosen ones, who cry out to him day and night? Will he keep putting them off? I tell you, he will see that they get justice, and quickly. However, when the Son of Man comes, will he find faith on the earth?"

Comment

1 There are a number of difficulties in our understanding of this parable. Righting of wrongs in this world seems to be anything but swift and speedy.

2 The parable is about unanswered prayers. The point is not that God does not care. The crooked judge is not held up as an example of what God does, only that it seems that way. God hears and answers in his own way and in his own time. Consider what kind of world we would have if all we had to do was pray and everything would be put right. We have to consider the parable a little more carefully.

3 The point of the parable is that we must continue in prayer even when it seems that heaven is deaf to our pleas.

4 This is one of the "how much more" kinds of story that Jesus used on more than one occasion. If a selfish and crooked judge will eventually grant the request of a needy widow, how much more will God our heavenly Father, the righteous judge of all the earth, help those who seek his help?

5 But God must not show his hand too obviously. If good was raised up and evil slapped down as and whenever it occurs, there would be no evil in the world, but there would be no real good either We would have no choice in the matter;

A Stroll Through the Bible

we would be machines, not God's children. So as the Scottish divine is reported to have explained this matter to his congregation, "God has to go about his business quietly."

6 Moses, called to lead God's people from Egypt to the promised land, asked for assurance from God that he was really was with him. So he asked to see God face to face. This was not considered possible, but God hid Moses in the cleft of a rock, and he was allowed to see God's back after he had passed by (Exod 33). We cannot see what God is doing right now in advance, but afterward we can often see what he has been doing behind the scenes. When we have been through bad and even terrible times, we can look back and see how God in his mercy has helped us and even used the trouble for our benefit.

7 A very good example of this is the troubles in Northern Ireland, an early example of the world-wide terrorism that was to come. It was a terrible time, but it accomplished something that had long been deemed impossible. It brought together the bulk of the Protestant and Catholic populations of the province, previously hopelessly at variance with one another, as fellow Christians. Study groups—including Protestant minsters and priests, church members, lay brothers, and nuns—were formed to study the Bible together to the great pleasure and benefit of all of them, who rediscovered the Bible and themselves in a new way. There are still some holdouts on either side, but the vast majority (around 80% in one survey) are moving forward together with a new understanding of one another as fellow Christians.

8 God moves mysteriously, but he moves nevertheless, and so we need to learn to keep praying and believing, learning the great Bible virtue of patience.

9 The last comment must be on the final verse in the parable: "When the Son of Man comes, will he find faith on the earth?" Here is the true humanity of Jesus: He was subject to all our problems, though without sin; he grieved at the stubbornness and lack of faith so common with us that it seems almost universal and unavoidable. The difference of this from our disappointment is that it was a momentary thought, not a continued attitude. Jesus had temptations of a very human kind in the wilderness at the beginning of his ministry, but he did not yield to them. And neither should we. So-called "doubting Thomas" has given us a good example, passing from questioning Jesus' resurrection to herculean faith, casting aside all his doubts and saying, "My Lord and my God."

The Prodigal Son

Luke 15:11-32

A Stroll Through the Bible

Jesus continued: "There was a man who had two sons. The younger one said to his father, 'Father, give me my share of the estate.' So he divided his property between them.

"Not long after that, the younger son got together all he had, set off for a distant country and there squandered his wealth in wild living. After he had spent everything, there was a severe famine in that whole country, and he began to be in need. So he went and hired himself out to a citizen of that country, who sent him to his fields to feed pigs. He longed to fill his stomach with the pods that the pigs were eating, but no one gave him anything.

"When he came to his senses, he said, 'How many of my father's hired servants have food to spare, and here I am starving to death! I will set out and go back to my father and say to him: Father, I have sinned against heaven and against you. I am no longer worthy to be called your son; make me like one of your hired servants.' So he got up and went to his father. (vv. 11-20)

Read through verse 32 in your Bible.

Comment

1 Like many stories in the Bible, this one is misnamed, for it is not about one person but three, the father and his two sons (and, most importantly, the Father). This is probably the best-known and best-loved parable, for it reveals the heart of the Father and his response to his rebellious children. There is, of course, retribution built into the way of the rebel, as with mankind in general. As the book of Proverbs says, "The way of the transgressor is hard" (13:15), and the wastrel soon begins to be in want, especially when a famine hits the far country and food becomes scarce. And this is also true in life generally. The broad road that leads to destruction quickly becomes hard and thorny and leads nowhere good. But God is a saving God, who mourns for the rebels and longs to see them back where they belong: in his family.

2 The theme of this parable is common to several religious traditions. There is no immediate example in the Jewish Talmud, but the theme of the loving and restoring God is found in various forms, as one would expect since the rabbis were constantly referring to and interpreting the Old Testament (cf. Hosea and his unfaithful wife). There is even a somewhat similar Buddhist tale in the Mahayana, though there is no reason to assume that either has influenced the other.

3 The younger son, the dissolute wastrel, has a glimmer of sense and draws the right conclusion from his troubles: that he would be better off at home even as a day laborer than starving to death where he is. And so he set off for home. This coming to oneself can be found in even the most depraved and wicked people. Quite a few Northern Ireland terrorists on both sides, who had killed and maimed many innocent people, came to themselves and became Christians and forces for good. We need to remember this when we are dealing with the terrorist menace. The immediate goal is national security. The ultimate goal is salvation and peace.

4 The younger son, the rake, had planned in advance what he would say to his father: "I am no longer worthy to be called your son." But the meeting was quite different. His father saw him returning when he was a long way off and ran to meet him, fell on his neck, kissed him, and made preparations for a grand celebration. And this happens when we come to ourselves; we find ourselves welcomed back, and it's party time. One young student from a very wealthy family who had enjoyed himself accordingly, when he had finally given over his life to Christ, told a friend, "I never had fun like this." A different quality of fun but better.

5 The elder brother, sour and resentful, represents well the harsh, self-righteous person found often in literature and also in daily life. The younger brother was separated from his father when he left home. The older one stayed home and was still separated from his father. They were not on the same page. Richard Baxter (1613–1691), Puritan preacher and theologian, advised preachers to "look lovingly on your congregation and with hope." With God, nobody is hopeless.

6 Notice that the elder brother described the returning wastrel as "this son of yours." The father in response describes him as "this brother of yours."

7 Note that the young rake, though restored as a son, still had a price to pay for his reckless escapade. He had spent his inheritance. He had eaten his cake and could not expect to still have it. There is a well-known Spanish proverb that goes, "Take what you want, but then pay for it." The father told the older brother that "you are always with me and all that I possess is yours." What on earth would the younger son do when his father died? One might hope that his older brother would have a change of heart and employ him perhaps as a manager. Who knows?

8 Campbell University Law School in North Carolina has an interesting "juvenile justice" program that deals mainly with children who have encountered trouble in school. The traditional way to deal with these kids is to expel them

from school, either temporarily or permanently, and, in more serious cases, to report them to the police. They then get introduced to the criminal justice system, seldom a nice experience. These cases often center on serious fights that are disruptive to the school and can lead to bad relationships, which are equally disruptive. Professor Jon Powell, who heads up the program, characterizes the legal response as punitive and the program's approach as restorative. He and his student helpers talk to the parties separately at first and then, if all goes well, encourage them to meet together along with the team and talk the matter over. In most cases the parties sort out their differences, shake hands, and return to the classroom as friends.

The Good Samaritan

Luke 10:25-37

On one occasion an expert in the law stood up to test Jesus. "Teacher," he asked, "what must I do to inherit eternal life?"

"What is written in the Law?" he replied. "How do you read it?"

He answered, "'Love the Lord your God with all your heart and with all your soul and with all your strength and with all your mind'; and, 'Love your neighbor as yourself.'"

"You have answered correctly," Jesus replied. "Do this and you will live."

But he wanted to justify himself, so he asked Jesus, "And who is my neighbor?" (vv. 25-29)

Read through verse 37 in your Bible.

Comment

1 The context of this episode is a long-standing enmity between the Jews and the Samaritans. When the Assyrians deported most of the population of Israel, the northern kingdom, those left behind intermarried with new people brought in by the Assyrians to take their place. These newcomers quickly assimilated with the local population and indeed considered themselves Israelites. But the Jews returning to Judaea, the southern kingdom, from Babylon considered them as being of mixed race and so foreigners. Also, they were living in Samaria, where the inhabitants had worshiped false gods. The Samaritans reacted to this hostile treatment in kind, so a deep hatred existed between the two communities. Samaria lay between Judaea and Galilee, and such was the hostility of the Jews toward the Samaritans that if they had to travel between Jerusalem and Galilee, they would go by the much longer way, east across the Jordan, bypassing Samaria. As was said in the story of the woman at the well (John 4), "the Jews have no dealings with the Samaritans."

2 The immediate occasion was a question from the lawyer to Jesus about which was the most important one among the great mass of the laws of Moses. Jesus replied with the *Shema*: "Hear, O Israel, the Lord thy God is one." The lawyer approved but wanted to allow limits to loving your neighbor as yourself, so he asked, "Who is my neighbor?" and would have been surprised if anyone suggested that a Samaritan might be included. Hence the story.

3 Who, according to Jesus, is your neighbor? Is the answer anybody who needs you? Or is it even wider in its application so that our enemies are our neighbors too? The answer would appear to be "yes" since we are to love our enemies. St. Paul instructed us, "If it is possible, as far as it depends on you, live at peace with everyone" (Rom 12:18).

4 We need to ask ourselves the same questions: Who are our enemies, and how should we treat them as our neighbors? We have many divisions in our world and in our own society, and we are inclined to treat those who differ from us as mortal enemies. It is the old division of people between "them" and "us." In *Gulliver's Travels*, Jonathan Swift describes two parties in a bitter political debate over which end of the boiled egg should be opened. One side said the large end and the other the smaller end. Many bitter human divisions boil down to similar insignificant differences.

The Sower and the Seed

Mark 4:1-20

Again Jesus began to teach by the lake. The crowd that gathered around him was so large that he got into a boat and sat in it out on the lake, while all the people were along the shore at the water's edge. He taught them many things by parables, and in his teaching said: "Listen! A farmer went out to sow his seed. As he was scattering the seed, some fell along the path, and the birds came and ate it up. Some fell on rocky places, where it did not have much soil. It sprang up quickly, because the soil was shallow. But when the sun came up, the plants were scorched, and they withered because they had no root. Other seed fell among thorns, which grew up and choked the plants, so that they did not bear grain. Still other seed fell on good soil. It came up, grew and produced a crop, some multiplying thirty, some sixty, some a hundred times."

Then Jesus said, "Whoever has ears to hear, let them hear." (vv. 1-9)

Comment

1 This parable should be called the parable of the soils because it describes how different people respond when the good news is presented to them. Some are like the hard-trodden pathways at the side of the field. They do not let the word into their hearts at all; in short, it has fallen on deaf ears. The seed on the shallow soil on top of a rock springs up very quickly, but it is not deep-rooted and withers away at the first sign of trouble. These are people who listen and respond to the word with enthusiasm but not wholeheartedly. They have not considered the changes it may require in the way they live their lives. They have only reached out for the benefits it seems to offer and not considered the cost. They are superficial in their faith, and when the cost shows up, in difficulty or opposition where endurance is required, they fade away. The third group hears and receives the word but becomes so involved in their business or other projects that the good word gets marginalized and ultimately squeezed out. Like the seed planted in thorny ground, it gets choked and withers away. God must come first. The real hearers let the good word deep into their hearts and lives and produce good crops.

2 Thinking of the shallow soil (on the rock), I remember a conversation with two people in their early twenties who were staunch believers in "once saved,

always saved." They both insisted that they could not imagine a situation where they would want to leave the faith; for different reasons, both later did. St. Paul warned his hearers against overconfidence: "If you think you are standing firm, be careful that you don't fall!" (1 Cor 10:12). We must let the good seed deep into our hearts and lives, then put on the whole armor of God and stand in the battle line.

3 Contrast with this the response of the wealthy tax collector Zacchaeus, who, after Jesus had visited him in his home, stood up and announced that he was going to give half of his wealth to the poor and refund fourfold anyone he had cheated. There was nothing shallow or superficial about his response to Jesus. He meant business and was pronounced a true son of Abraham; he was "in."

4 It is one thing to stand up and take the marriage vows "for better, for worse, etc." but another thing to stand by your life's partner in bodily or mental sickness or serious financial hardship or temptation to stray. People who take those vows seriously dig in their heels and can endure incredibly hard times, and they reap the rewards of their faithfulness.

5 This parable applies to almost every situation and every project and every profession you could think of, including the Christian ministry. We must expect hardship. Few, if any, get an easy run through life: "We must go through many hardships to enter the kingdom of God" (Acts 14:22). But as we endure, like good soldiers of Jesus Christ, we are surely rewarded both in this life and in the life to come. And we inevitably become fruitful; through us God's kingdom is extended.

The Parable of the Talents

Matthew 25:14-30

"Again, it will be like a man going on a journey, who called his servants and entrusted his wealth to them. To one he gave five bags of gold, to another two bags, and to another one bag, each according to his ability. Then he went on his journey. The man who had received five bags of gold went at once and put his money to work and gained five bags more. So also, the one with two bags of gold gained two more. But the man who had received one bag went off, dug a hole in the ground and hid his master's money. (vv. 14-18)

Read through verse 30 in your Bible.

Comment

1 The servant who was given only one talent has traditionally been seen as someone with very limited ability. Nothing could be further from the truth. A talent of silver weighs 36 kg (80 lbs) and is worth more than half a million dollars in today's money, which means that even the least talented of us is overloaded with abilities.

2 The idle servant was not cast into the outer darkness because he did anything bad, but because he had not done anything at all with his talent. The implication for us is obvious: We are put into this world to become God's servants. God does not do his work with machines but with people. So even if we have never been drunk or stolen money or been unkind to children or animals or done any of the other things that are considered bad, we may still be condemned because, like the lazy servant, we had not done what we were supposed to do, using and multiplying our talents to the glory of God.

3 Eusebius, bishop of Caesarea in the fourth century AD, records in his *The Church History* another Gospel written in Hebrew (now lost) with a different account of the parable. Only the servant with two talents is rewarded, and the big villain, who was pitched into the outer darkness, was not the one-talent man but the five-talent servant who had wasted the talents on women, booze, and whatever. I think the Synoptic version is more likely to be the original. It is certainly the more profound.

4 The next question is, "What is God's work?" First, it is to believe in and accept his Son, Jesus, into our hearts and lives (John 6:29), then to go to work. This, in general, is not to work *for* God, but to work *with* God, doing whatever we may be called on to do. It includes what we do in our homes or work and opportunities to do good of any and every kind. God has some task for each one of us to carry out on any particular day; it might be small or great, but whatever it is, we must do it with all our might (Eccl 9:10).

5 A most important point to note is the reward that is promised. The servants were not given wealth or pleasure or glory, but a bigger job with more responsibility. We start low down in the Lord's business and use the talents we have on whatever comes to hand. As we get more experienced, we find that we have other and greater talents, and God puts them to work. Thus, we keep advancing in our assigned work and growing in our abilities. The way to find God's will for your life is to get busy with the things that lie under your hand and go from there. Dwight L. Moody was a shoe salesman when he first came to faith, and he decided to be the very best shoe salesman he could be. He soon noticed lots of children in the streets of Chicago who had no connection with any church, so he opened a Sunday school and walked around the streets collecting children, for he did not feel able to teach them. Eventually, a teacher did not show up, so he had to fill in and found he could do it. Things progressed in this manner until he became the best-known and respected evangelist of his day. He later opened the Moody Bible Institute, which is still going strong. In the Lord's army, privates quickly become corporals, then sergeants, and eventually even generals and field marshals. But no promotion can be higher than that given to Moses, who was called the servant (literally the slave) of God.

The Parable about Unfair Treatment

Matthew 20:1-16

"For the kingdom of heaven is like a landowner who went out early in the morning to hire workers for his vineyard. He agreed to pay them a denarius for the day and sent them into his vineyard.

"About nine in the morning he went out and saw others standing in the marketplace doing nothing. He told them, 'You also go and work in my vineyard, and I will pay you whatever is right.' So they went. (vv. 1-5)

Read through verse 16 in your Bible.

Comment

1 This parable reminds us of a modern trade dispute with the one-hour workers being paid and the rest protesting, carrying signs that read, "Vineyard unfair to workers."

2 The all-day workers had a point. It wasn't fair to give the same amount to those who only worked one hour when they had toiled all day in the heat.

3 The context of the parable is that the Jews who had toiled and suffered through their long history felt that they were special, better than the Gentiles and tax collectors and prostitutes who were only lately being admitted into the kingdom of God by Jesus.

4 Jesus' point in this parable is that citizenship in the kingdom is not a reward for services rendered but a free gift from a generous God. The only qualification is to be willing to accept it along with Jesus, who is both the giver and the gift.

5 Truly saintly persons understand this. Uniformly, they feel that they did not deserve God's wonderful gift, for a gift it was. They are not being rewarded for their good living but being provided with a new heart to live differently, so as to please God and help their fellow creatures. One of the many saintly persons I have been privileged to know was Dr. Charles Howard. Dr. Howard was a Baptist preacher, a mighty one with a national reputation, who received very little of this world's goods for his services. He had managed to save up enough money to buy an engagement ring for his betrothed, Alma, but a young man who hoped to

become a preacher needed money for a down payment to a college. Charles and Alma discussed the matter, and she said they didn't need a ring and to give the money to the young man. They did, and this was the beginning of the Howard Christian Education Fund. The recipients returned the money, usually with interest, and it grew to be a multimillion-dollar enterprise. An investigative reporter was sent down to report on it. He arrived, convinced it was a scam. He ended up giving a donation to the fund himself. In short, Dr. Howard was a wonderful and saintly man if ever there was one. But he did not see himself that way. Generally speaking, he felt he was the worst sinner in the county, if not the state. It is always so: the saints do not feel worthy, only extremely grateful.

The Surpassing Value of God's Kingdom

Matthew 13:44-46

"The kingdom of heaven is like treasure hidden in a field. When a man found it, he hid it again, and then in his joy went and sold all he had and bought that field.

"Again, the kingdom of heaven is like a merchant looking for fine pearls. When he found one of great value, he went away and sold everything he had and bought it."

Comment

1 These two parables are about the cost of being a servant of Christ, which can be considerable, but the message is that even if it takes all that we have and all that we are, it is well worth it.

2 We are all aware these days that Christians all over the world pay with their lives, choosing to be loyal to their Master.

3 Christians in Communist Russia or in other countries hostile to the Christian faith had to sacrifice their education or their careers if they chose to take their stand and be known as Christians. But they did so and felt they had chosen well.

4 In the West we have not reached such a pitch of hostility to the faith, but there is a price to be paid here nevertheless. We may lose friends and positions in society and instead get constant critical scrutiny. Where he has the power to do it, the old enemy will try to hurt us and probably succeed.

5 Some of us are thick in the skin, so abuse and ridicule don't bother us much. Nobody bullied Charles Wesley in school, or they risked a thick ear or worse. His brother John was another story. John Wesley had some bullying in school, but it was nothing to the treatment he and his preachers had to put up with later. Many of them were killed by mobs, led on occasion by the local parish minister. And they did so cheerfully and with humor. When a thug barred John Wesley's path and said, "I never make way for a fool," Wesley stepped aside and said, "I always do." And as we stand firm, we often find support from surprising quarters. In Thomas Hughes' great novel *Tom Brown's Schooldays*, little Arthur, the delicate son of a clergyman, kneeled down at his bedside in the dormitory to say his

prayers on his first night in public school. Immediately, somebody shied a boot at him and jeered. But Arthur's courage made the tough Tom Brown ashamed of himself that he had given in to the common careless practice, and right away he made it clear to the scoffers that if they didn't quit, they would have a fight on their hands, and nobody wanted to fight Tom Brown. Even if you licked him, you would be sorry you took him on. The old hymn tells us to stand up for Jesus, and if we do, it strengthens the hand of others around us and can even herald a change in public attitudes.

6 Following a discussion recorded in Luke 18 about how hard it is for rich people to enter the kingdom of heaven, Peter said to Jesus, "We have left our own homes and followed you." Peter was perhaps expecting to be praised, but Jesus responded, "There is no one who has left house or wife or brothers or parents or children for the sake of the kingdom of God who will not receive many times as much at this time and in the age to come, eternal life." God is nobody's debtor; even in this life the rewards of being a Christian far outweigh any suffering or loss we may meet. And of course in the world to come there is the greatest prize of all: the gift of eternal life with Christ in heaven.

7 A current ridiculous commercial for Stella Artois, a Belgian beer, features a young man who just heard they were going bankrupt. So he piles all his possessions on a bicycle and holds an auction so he can buy the brewery and keep it going. Silly, but the same idea.

The Parable of the Rich Fool

Luke 12:13-21

Someone in the crowd said to him, "Teacher, tell my brother to divide the inheritance with me."

Jesus replied, "Man, who appointed me a judge or an arbiter between you?" Then he said to them, "Watch out! Be on your guard against all kinds of greed; life does not consist in an abundance of possessions."

And he told them this parable: "The ground of a certain rich man yielded an abundant harvest. He thought to himself, 'What shall I do? I have no place to store my crops.'

"Then he said, 'This is what I'll do. I will tear down my barns and build bigger ones, and there I will store my surplus grain. And I'll say to myself, "You have plenty of grain laid up for many years. Take life easy; eat, drink and be merry."'

"But God said to him, 'You fool! This very night your life will be demanded from you. Then who will get what you have prepared for yourself?'

"This is how it will be with whoever stores up things for themselves but is not rich toward God."

Comment

1 What was the rich man doing wrong, and why was he called a fool? He was not stupid. Indeed, many people would say he must have been smart to have farmed so well and to know how to manage his wealth. But his focus was too narrow. He was only thinking of wealth, which is a good thing in itself, better than poverty or debt or starving. However, it is neither the only nor the most important thing in life, as bad circumstances can quickly reveal. His life was pointless.

2. Some old miser jokes make this point:

• A miser advising his son told him that money was not everything; health was the other five percent.

• A robber put a pistol to a rich man's head and said, "Your money or your life." His victim replied, "Let me think about that for a minute."

- An Irish farmer had always been hammering it into his son to be sure to marry for money rather than love. The son finally brought a lady home for his dad's approval. Father was appalled. "Son," he said, "I know I told you to marry for money, but this one is just too awful." (He listed the numerous disgusting defects of the lady.) "You don't need to whisper," his son said. "She's deaf too."

The point of these old stories—and there are lots of them—is that even a miser has to see that there is more to life than wealth.

3 This also applies with equal force to other forms of wealth, such as fame and reputation, success and social position. They melt into nothingness when confronted with life's tragedies (and who can avoid them forever?). Consider serious illness; worse still, the life-threatening illness of a loved one, say a child; financial ruin or loss of one's previously good reputation; collapse of some enterprise, small or large, that we had spent half our life building. In the face of these things, common enough, all earth's treasures are seen to have little value. They crumble into dust.

4 Even in the absence of tragic events, here is one thing that gives all of us pause to think of the worthwhileness (or lack thereof) in whatever we have done or accumulated over the years. It is the grim reaper, the old man with the scythe, who calls on us to hand over the keys to our desk and depart. At that time many forms of wealth suddenly become unimportant, and we have to consider what we have done with the life God gave us.

5 The pointlessness of an ordinary life, even a busy and apparently successful one, is depressing. I think that is what bothered Gautama Buddha when he saw three bad things in one day. Missionaries tell me that this sadness about a pointless existence is prevalent in the Far Eastern cultures and a more powerful motivation to accept Christ rather than a sense of sin. Jesus told us that the inhabitants of Sodom and Gomorrah, the cities of the plain that were about to be destroyed, were totally immersed in their ordinary affairs. There has to be something more to life than getting and begetting, toiling, and all the other necessities of our ordinary existence.

6 The final accounting of the worth of our lives is a troublesome business to the best of us, and the best that the most case-hardened among us can do is to accept our fate stoically. But truly great people have been haunted by the feeling that they had not achieved what they should have, that the sum total of their lives

did not amount to much. But this is as it should be. The important thing is not what we have done, but what God does with it. The little boy who handed over his lunch to Jesus had no idea what a great thing the Master would be able to do with it. It is the same with the littlest thing we offer to our Lord. John Wesley, dying after one of the busiest and most productive lives anyone could imagine, said, "What hath God wrought?" His efforts were trivial in comparison to what God made out of them.

7 St. Paul said, "Whatever you do, whether in word or deed, do it all in the name of the Lord Jesus" (Col 3:17), which means that anything we do, however small and apparently trivial, if it is offered to God and done for his sake, will never be wasted. We will also be laying up treasure in heaven, where moth and rust do not destroy and thieves cannot break in and steal (Matt 6:20).

Getting Rid of an Undesirable Tenant

Matthew 12:38-45

Then some of the Pharisees and teachers of the law said to him, "Teacher, we want to see a sign from you."

He answered, "A wicked and adulterous generation asks for a sign! But none will be given it except the sign of the prophet Jonah. For as Jonah was three days and three nights in the belly of a huge fish, so the Son of Man will be three days and three nights in the heart of the earth. The men of Nineveh will stand up at the judgment with this generation and condemn it; for they repented at the preaching of Jonah, and now something greater than Jonah is here. The Queen of the South will rise at the judgment with this generation and condemn it; for she came from the ends of the earth to listen to Solomon's wisdom, and now something greater than Solomon is here.

"When an impure spirit comes out of a person, it goes through arid places seeking rest and does not find it. Then it says, 'I will return to the house I left.' When it arrives, it finds the house unoccupied, swept clean and put in order. Then it goes and takes with it seven other spirits more wicked than itself, and they go in and live there. And the final condition of that person is worse than the first. That is how it will be with this wicked generation."

Comment

1 The background of this strange parable is the violent response of the scribes and Pharisees and rulers of the Jews to the teaching of Jesus, especially where he reinterpreted the Law of Moses. A mere human had no right to do this, but Jesus was even worse. He claimed to be the divine Messiah and showed this by his amazing teaching with identifying miracles to back it up. But even the raising of Lazarus from the dead was not enough to bring these authorities over; in fact, it made them all the more eager to kill Jesus since they were afraid that everyone would be encouraged to revolt from the rule of the Romans, who would then intervene and take away their power and authority, which was considerable under Roman rule. As the old proverb puts it, "There are none so blind as those who don't want to see."

2 Jesus characterizes their religion as "do-it-yourself," deciding to keep all the details of the rules and regulations of Moses, the outward things, but neglecting or ignoring the more important inward things. Jesus called it cleaning the outside of the cup but leaving the dirty inside untouched (Matt 23:25).

3 This parable of the haunted house describes the results of do-it-yourself improvement schemes. This is a superficial way to get rid of a deeper problem, As Jeremiah puts it, God's law must be written in the innermost part of our being, the heart, and God himself must write it there. We do not get better by reform but by inward renewal by the spirit of God.

4 Several young people I came across told me they were unhappy with themselves and had decided to make themselves over physically, mentally, and spiritually. I think it wore off after a bit. The desired new condition did not appear in any satisfactory manner. Reform is not renewal.

5 Think for a moment of the parable of the sower and the various soils. The seed sewn on the shallow soil sprang up quickly but withered away. Only the seed planted deeply in the good soil, in the heart, produced fruit.

6 But how is this to happen? Not by doing, but by receiving. And not just passive receiving, but rather by welcoming into our hearts the risen Savior, who is always knocking on the door and who will come in, start cleaning up the mess, and live in it with us.

The Coming of the Holy Spirit

Acts 2

When the day of Pentecost came, they were all together in one place. Suddenly a sound like the blowing of a violent wind came from heaven and filled the whole house where they were sitting. They saw what seemed to be tongues of fire that separated and came to rest on each of them. All of them were filled with the Holy Spirit and began to speak in other tongues as the Spirit enabled them. (vv. 1-4)

Read through verse 21 in your Bible.

Comment

1 The speaking in tongues mentioned here is not the same as that found in the rest of the New Testament—the *glossolalia*, where nobody knew what they were talking about unless someone interpreted. This was different—a miraculous happening where everybody heard what was said in their own native language. It was a typical "sign," a teaching miracle, showing the commissioning of the church to preach the good news to all people.

2 It is noteworthy that although prophecy was the most important order in the church ministry, the daughters were included along with the sons. There was no gender preference in the gift of prophecy. Philip the evangelist had four daughters, all prophets (Acts 21:9). Prophets were not ordained by the church but called by God and spoke as from God. When a prophet came into a church meeting, the normal order of service was suspended until the prophet had delivered whatever message they had received from God.

3 Some churches, not all of them Pentecostal, still retain the idea of speaking in tongues. It was certainly common in the apostolic age and has appeared here and there among other denominations today. I only heard it once and was unimpressed. The preacher periodically rolled his eyes up and repeated several times "shalom babeluk" (and nobody interpreted). St. Paul, by the way, had to rein in the practice, insisting that if there was not an interpreter to explain the meaning of the message, it should not be allowed in the church but kept for private use in one's own room. This is the rule in Pentecostal churches, but it is frequently broken, and the pastor who tries to stop it can face backlash. There are also a number of Pentecostal congregations, one of them not far from my home, who while

believing in being filled with the Spirit, do not have the *glossolalia.* I have several friends who speak in tongues, but only in their own rooms during their private times of prayer. They tell me they are so overcome with praise that ordinary language fails and God gives them a special tongue.

4 It is interesting that in the list of the offices in the church, there is no mention of preachers. And I think the reason for this is that they were called by another name—prophets—and they did not necessarily speak in tongues. They lived close to God, heard his word, and proclaimed it to the church. Often the messages that they proclaimed were predictions, and certainly these would be the ones remembered and recorded. But Samuel and the others had more than one kind of message: warnings and instructions of all sorts and varieties. This is what a preacher is and should be: one who listens to God, receives a message, and then passes it on. This is what ordinary preachers try to do. But when they have been given the message, perhaps a passage or a story from the Bible, glorious and blazing with heavenly light, there is more to do. They have to go to work and figure out how best to deliver it.

Paul Shipwrecked

Acts 27:27-44

On the fourteenth night we were still being driven across the Adriatic Sea, when about midnight the sailors sensed they were approaching land. They took soundings and found that the water was a hundred and twenty feet deep. A short time later they took soundings again and found it was ninety feet deep. Fearing that we would be dashed against the rocks, they dropped four anchors from the stern and prayed for daylight. In an attempt to escape from the ship, the sailors let the lifeboat down into the sea, pretending they were going to lower some anchors from the bow. Then Paul said to the centurion and the soldiers, "Unless these men stay with the ship, you cannot be saved." So the soldiers cut the ropes that held the lifeboat and let it drift away. (vv. 27-32)

Read through verse 44 in your Bible.

Comment

1 Paul, when listing the hardships and disasters that had happened to him in his service for Christ, mentions two shipwrecks, but only one is described in Acts. The Mediterranean is subject to sudden violent storms, and its floor is studded with wrecked ships, some of them very interesting as to their construction and cargoes.

2 Notice Paul's composure in disasters, very impressive to the other passengers who did not have his faith and tended to panic. There have been innumerable examples of this since. John Wesley was impressed by the fact that even the Moravian children were not afraid in a similar situation. As the *Titanic* was sinking, crew and passengers who were Christians were likewise calm and unmoved. The Christian martyrs, from St. Stephen to the present time, know how to keep their heads, as Rudyard Kipling's poem "If" put it, "when all around are losing theirs."

3 St. Paul, as always, was ready to turn an event into an opportunity to tell people about Christ. He was singularly successful here. He met with the governor of Malta and put in a good word there too. The church in Malta had its beginnings with this visit and has had a great history since that time.

4 Paul's courageous behavior here, both during the storm and following the wreck, must have given a powerful impetus to his words. And this is always the case. People take notice of us and may indeed ask us, or inquire of others, why we do what we do and behave as we behave.

5 We can learn several good lessons from St. Paul's record here: first, to meet disasters and bad things with God and so be of good cheer; and even while frightening things are going on, to think of others rather than ourselves; and finally to use every occasion to speak a good word for the Master.

A Midnight Prayer-meeting in Jail

Acts 16:16-40

About midnight Paul and Silas were praying and singing hymns to God, and the other prisoners were listening to them. Suddenly there was such a violent earthquake that the foundations of the prison were shaken. At once all the prison doors flew open, and everyone's chains came loose. The jailer woke up, and when he saw the prison doors open, he drew his sword and was about to kill himself because he thought the prisoners had escaped. But Paul shouted, "Don't harm yourself! We are all here!"

The jailer called for lights, rushed in and fell trembling before Paul and Silas. He then brought them out and asked, "Sirs, what must I do to be saved?"

They replied, "Believe in the Lord Jesus, and you will be saved—you and your household." Then they spoke the word of the Lord to him and to all the others in his house. At that hour of the night the jailer took them and washed their wounds; then immediately he and all his household were baptized. The jailer brought them into his house and set a meal before them; he was filled with joy because he had come to believe in God—he and his whole household. (vv. 25-34)

Comment

1 The most obvious question here is "What did Paul and Silas have to praise God for?" They had been whipped with the Roman flagellum. They were in a filthy prison, which was hardly making their wounded backs more comfortable. They were chained hand and foot, as jailers in those times were terrified because if any of their prisoners escaped, they were given their punishment. Yet in pain, dirt, and discomfort they were singing and praising God. It must have been a most unusual sound in the jail at Philippi.

2 The obvious reason is that Paul had an odd way of looking at such things: "We also glory in our sufferings, because we know that suffering produces perseverance" (Rom 5:3). Christians can glory in trouble because they know God is right there with them, turning evil into good and providing opportunities for spreading the good word as people see how differently they deal with trouble.

3 It was so here. God delivered them with a timely earthquake, which burst open the doors and tore all the chains out of the walls.

4 The natural response of prisoners in these circumstances is to make a run for it; their future was not usually bright where they were. But Paul and Silas were concerned for the jailer, who would be in big trouble if any prisoners escaped.

5 The episode must have been terrifying for the jailer. The simultaneous events of an earthquake and the bursting open of the jail surely unnerved the poor man and made him think in terms of God and eternity, especially if he had heard Paul preaching.

6 A frightening event can shake us out of our preoccupation with day-to-day duties and happenings. We have to deal with these everyday things, but they should not blind us to more important matters. Many a person has, in a crisis, suddenly realized the relative unimportance of the daily mixture of grind and relaxation to think more deeply about life and its meaning.

7 And when Paul had preached the word of the Lord to the jailer and all in his house, they were all baptized, and the jailer rejoiced with all his house that they had believed in God. It is always so, for receiving salvation is a most joyful experience. As a young student commented on his conversion to Christ, "I have never had so much fun in my life".

Letters of St. Paul: Faith, Hope, and Love

1 Corinthians 13

If I speak in the tongues of men or of angels, but do not have love, I am only a resounding gong or a clanging cymbal. If I have the gift of prophecy and can fathom all mysteries and all knowledge, and if I have a faith that can move mountains, but do not have love, I am nothing. If I give all I possess to the poor and give over my body to hardship that I may boast, but do not have love, I gain nothing.

Love is patient, love is kind. It does not envy, it does not boast, it is not proud. It does not dishonor others, it is not self-seeking, it is not easily angered, it keeps no record of wrongs. Love does not delight in evil but rejoices with the truth. It always protects, always trusts, always hopes, always perseveres.

Love never fails. But where there are prophecies, they will cease; where there are tongues, they will be stilled; where there is knowledge, it will pass away. For we know in part and we prophesy in part, but when completeness comes, what is in part disappears. When I was a child, I talked like a child, I thought like a child, I reasoned like a child. When I became a man, I put the ways of childhood behind me. For now we see only a reflection as in a mirror; then we shall see face to face. Now I know in part; then I shall know fully, even as I am fully known.

And now these three remain: faith, hope and love. But the greatest of these is love.

Comment

1 The background of this famous passage, the hymn to love, is in the previous chapter where Paul was discussing the *glossolalia*. We all tend to be impressed with more spectacular and publicly appreciated gifts, and speaking in tongues had become vastly overvalued and indeed was an embarrassment to the church, as visitors coming in and hearing such performances might well think that the Christians were mad or drunk. Speaking in tongues should therefore be confined to private devotions or, if in public, must be accompanied by an interpretation either by the speaker or some other person. The customary absence of such interpretation commonly means the virtual abandonment of the *glossolalia* in church services. There is nothing wrong with the practice in private devotions when the Spirit is present in such power that ordinary speech is inadequate. This is how modern Pentecostals tend to describe their gift of a tongue.

2 Paul shows us what he calls a better way to know that the Holy Spirit has entered our lives and is in charge. He sees the essential activity of the Holy Spirit in us as producing three things: faith, hope, and love.

3 True faith, an overpowering confidence that Christ and his gospel are really and reliably true, is the work of the Spirit and an assurance for us that we are in Christ and that he is in and operative in us. John Wesley, in his account of his famous Aldersgate experience, found that he did indeed trust God and Christ alone for his salvation. And we too, when the faith burns brightly in us, can likewise know that the Spirit is at work. Indeed, by and by, the faith is so usual with us that we can feel, as we go about our daily duties, that like Enoch of old, we are walking with God (Gen 5:24).

4 Hope is a great word in the Bible generally and especially in St. Paul's letters, for we do not live by sight or by absolute mathematical certainty; we are always looking for some fulfillment of one sort or another in the future. Hope is the fruit of two things: faith and experience. The stronger our faith, the more certainly we hope, and with experience our faith is reinforced and we have more confidence in what we do (Rom 5:3-5). We are—if not by nature, by grace—optimists, not merely hoping for the best but expecting it, for God works all things (good and bad) for our benefit (Rom 8:28).

5 The third and greatest gift of the Holy Spirit is love. The New Testament word for love is *agape*. There are two other words for love in Greek: *philia*, commonly translated "friendship"; *eros*, used for various grades and kinds of romantic love

(captured by the term "erotic"). The three are used more or less interchangeably in Greek literature, but in the New Testament *agape* is used to translate *chesed*, the Hebrew word used for the persistent, enduring love of God for his wayward people Israel. Hosea uses it to express his love for his unfaithful wife, Gomer, who repeatedly took off after various lovers and commonly ended up abandoned and in slavery. But Hosea did not give up on her and kept buying her back (redeeming her) and bringing her home again. This is the picture of God we find in the parables of Jesus. The father continues to mourn for his prodigal son; the shepherd seeks his lost sheep; the woman keeps looking for the lost coin until she finds it; God is not like the unjust judge but listens to the prayers of his chosen ones. Christ's own attitude illustrates it perfectly. It shows in his treatment of the lost and social outcasts, such as sinners and tax collectors; his word to the robber on the cross; his thoughtfulness and consideration shown to the woman taken in adultery and heartlessly dragged into his presence to make trouble for him. One could go on for a long time listing Jesus' words and actions along these lines. If we want to know what love means in the Bible, we have only to look at the sayings and actions of Jesus. Love is the opposite of self-concern. It flows out in concern and kindness and generosity to other people. We find it in the reported experience of the lawyer frightened into the kingdom by the terrorist bombings on 9/11 who found, somewhat to his surprise, that his whole perspective on life and other people had been turned inside out. John Wesley reported on his Aldersgate experience (surely the Holy Spirit entering in and taking charge of his life) that he felt he loved the whole world.

One might well wonder whether such amazing things could ever happen to the likes of you and me. But Jesus told us not to be surprised, for if we, being far from as good as we should be, know how to give good gifts to our children, surely our heavenly Father will give the Holy Spirit to those who ask him for it (Luke 11:13).

Romans 5:1-11

Therefore, since we have been justified through faith, we have peace with God through our Lord Jesus Christ, through whom we have gained access by faith into this grace in which we now stand. And we boast in the hope of the glory of God. Not only so, but we also glory in our sufferings, because we know that suffering produces perseverance; perseverance, character; and character, hope. And hope does not put us to shame, because God's love has been poured out into our hearts through the Holy Spirit, who has been given to us.

You see, at just the right time, when we were still powerless, Christ died for the ungodly. Very rarely will anyone die for a righteous person, though for a good person someone might possibly dare to die. But God demonstrates his own love for us in this: While we were still sinners, Christ died for us.

Since we have now been justified by his blood, how much more shall we be saved from God's wrath through him! For if, while we were God's enemies, we

A Stroll Through the Bible

were reconciled to him through the death of his Son, how much more, having been reconciled, shall we be saved through his life! Not only is this so, but we also boast in God through our Lord Jesus Christ, through whom we have now received reconciliation.

Comment

1 *Peace* is a great word in the Bible. It translates *irene* in Greek and *shalom* in Hebrew. It does not mean merely the absence of war, a cessation of hostilities, as in a cease-fire, but a complete reconciliation between the parties, the restoration of good relations—in short, harmony.

2 The most basic peace is peace with God—no longer refusing him, battling with him, or running away from him. The curse on mankind of expulsion from the garden of Eden is then lifted, and we can once more walk and talk with God in the cool of the evening.

3 We can then be at peace with those around us, since peace with God brings a new attitude toward our fellow human beings. We want to help them, not hurt them or take something away from them.

4 Finally, we can be at peace with ourselves. When you are at odds with God, disorder reigns within. Jesus' parable of the empty house (Luke 11)—cleared of its resident devil only to be taken over by seven worse ones—is true to life. If God is not in residence and in charge, sooner or later (and probably sooner), the devils enter, inner conflict begins, and a general mess is on the way. When the Lord reenters, the demons are expelled, and there is blessed peace, harmony, and prosperity of every kind.

5 But note that this peace has been purchased for us at a fearful price. It was obtained by the terrible sacrifice of Christ for us on the cross. This is a great mystery, difficult for us to imagine much less understand, but we can appropriate its benefits and be thankful.

6 Paul makes it clear how we should do this. He tells us to confess with our mouth the Lord Jesus—in short, openly declare our allegiance, believe in our heart that he is risen and present with us; the result is salvation, peace with God, peace with man, and peace with ourselves (Rom 10:9).

St. Paul's Thorn in the Flesh—and Ours

2 Corinthians 12:7-9

Therefore, in order to keep me from becoming conceited, I was given a thorn in my flesh, a messenger of Satan, to torment me. Three times I pleaded with the Lord to take it away from me. But he said to me, "My grace is sufficient for you, for my power is made perfect in weakness." Therefore I will boast all the more gladly about my weaknesses, so that Christ's power may rest on me.

Comment

1 A thorn in our skin is not much to talk about. We can either pull it out ourselves or if it breaks off or is deeply embedded, we can go to a doctor's office or the emergency room of a hospital and have it removed (along with a tetanus shot perhaps). But in the Middle East there are large and nasty thorn bushes. The thorns were not easy to remove, and one might have to go around in some pain and discomfort for a time until the body sealed it off with scar tissue.

2 There has been much speculation as to what this thorn in the flesh was. Some have suggested facetiously that he had a termagant wife tucked away somewhere. Others have suggested spells of malaria, which prostrated him for several days at a time. A very likely possibility is epileptic seizures, which were then attributed to demon possession. Another possibility is a hasty temper or some other flare-up. But whatever it was, the point to note is that he was unable to get rid of it and had to learn to live with it.

3 There is a valuable lesson for us here. When we open the door and Jesus comes into our lives, we are a new creation. Old things are passed away, and all things have become new. But the details of this new creation have to be spelled out a little, for not everything is changed. Our physical appearance remains the same. If my face would stop a clock (as my sisters used to tell me), my countenance will not become any more becoming. Our other physical characteristics will remain the same also; even our disorders will continue unless we are one of those fortunate ones who is miraculously cured. What is changed is our attitude to these things and how we overcome our handicaps by God's grace in our daily lives. Helen Brookes, the wife of one of our Methodist ministers in Ireland, became blind early in life and prayed earnestly that the Lord would give her back her sight. It didn't happen, but God's grace gave her a wonderful gift of acting and living just

A Stroll Through the Bible

as if she could see. She became a walking miracle and a ministering angel to a great many people.

4 One of our most important characteristics is our personality, the basic traits that show themselves in our living and behavior. Some of us are timid; some tend to be rash and impulsive; some are easily offended, and some thick-skinned; some are outgoing and socially inclined, and others more introspective. The list of the varieties of our personal makeup is long, and by and large it remains with us until the end of our lives. We cannot change these things—the leopard cannot change its spots—but we can learn to live with them and overcome them. My friend and former dean was a quiet and persuasive person, collegial rather than imperative in his manner of administration. I was surprised when he showed up as a strongly dominant type on a personality test. He told me he had learned to live with it and make allowances for it in his decisions.

5 I knew a committed Christian, a teacher, who compared himself unfavorably with his headmaster, who was more or less godless but pleasant and agreeable. His conclusion was that his principal was a better Christian than he himself was. This was a wrong conclusion. The difference between him and his principal was a matter of temperament—the one was placid and the other choleric. People can get the benefit or the blame for their personality, which they did not earn but received as a benefit or the reverse. People with placid and benign personalities are often described as saints while Christians who are not so fortunate in their disposition are considered second-class, immature, even hypocrites.

6 All Christians are called "saints" in the New Testament, but the term must be understood properly. The word derives from *hagios* (ἅγιος,), meaning holy. But this adjective was used for anything that was consecrated for the service of God, even the vessels and other accoutrements in the temple—that is, they were God's property. It is in that sense that all Christians are called saints, for they have given themselves over to God and are his property. St. Paul did not tell misbehaving Christians they were no longer saints; he told them to be worthy of the name. To be God's property we must strive to share his character—to treat all people as God does, for he causes the rain to fall on the evil as well as the good and his sun to shine on the just and unjust alike (Matt 5:45).

7 . We need to get to know ourselves and learn to live with ourselves and manage the uncomely parts of our personality and ways of operating. God's grace is sufficient. We are God's possession, so we must then seek to become more like the one who possesses us.

St. Paul and the Future Life

2 Corinthians 5:1-10

For we know that if the earthly tent we live in is destroyed, we have a building from God, an eternal house in heaven, not built by human hands. Meanwhile we groan, longing to be clothed instead with our heavenly dwelling, because when we are clothed, we will not be found naked. For while we are in this tent, we groan and are burdened, because we do not wish to be unclothed but to be clothed instead with our heavenly dwelling, so that what is mortal may be swallowed up by life. Now the one who has fashioned us for this very purpose is God, who has given us the Spirit as a deposit, guaranteeing what is to come.

Therefore we are always confident and know that as long as we are at home in the body we are away from the Lord. For we live by faith, not by sight. We are confident, I say, and would prefer to be away from the body and at home with the Lord. So we make it our goal to please him, whether we are at home in the body or away from it. For we must all appear before the judgment seat of Christ, so that each of us may receive what is due us for the things done while in the body, whether good or bad.

Comment

1 This passage concerns the future life—in particular, heaven, the reward of the just. But it is prophetic language, and it is always important to remember the warning of the great Dr. J. Agar Beet that prophecy and the fulfillment of prophecy are two different things. When the fulfillment arrives, it is often not recognized by the people expecting it.

2 The idea of the afterlife did not appear fully fledged in the Bible. It developed slowly with time. Originally the realm of the dead, called *Sheol* in Hebrew, was a dark place under the earth and was simply the place where the dead lived in a sort of shadowy existence. Some of the books of the Old Testament, especially Job, go further than this, saying that at the end of time God, the only true judge, would raise the dead and reward each according to their works. In the meantime the dead slept. In the period between the Old and New Testaments, the idea developed that the waiting place should not be the same for the righteous as for the wrongdoers, so *Sheol* was divided into two parts: the place where the righteous dwelt, known as "Abraham's bosom"; and the other part, which was a place of torment (see Luke 16, the parable of the rich man and Lazarus). As always the final word is with Jesus, who said, "I am the resurrection and the life. The one who believes in me will live, even though they die; and whoever lives by believing in me will never die" (John 11:25-26). This is the basis for Christians believing they go straight to the presence of Christ in heaven when they die. We are excused from the final judgment day and enter heaven by a more direct route. Remember also what Jesus said to the penitent robber on the cross next to him: "Today you will be with me in paradise."

3 St. Paul describes our earthly body as a mere traveling tent to be replaced by a nobler body or dwelling in the presence of Christ. This is the biblical idea of the future life—not a bodiless existence, but a new and nobler body. St. Paul uses the analogy of the seed and the flower to explain this. The seed has a body suitable for living in the ground, but when it emerges in the flower, it has a new body suitable for living in the air and sunlight. As our present body is suitable for our earthly life, our future body will be suitable for a heavenly life (1 Cor 15:35-39).

4 As to the nature of this future life Paul, tells us, "What no eye has seen, what no ear has heard, and what no human mind has conceived—the things God has prepared for those who love him" (1 Cor 2:9). In short, it is so wonderful that it is unimaginable. We can only describe it by weak analogies, golden streets, heavenly music, etc.

5 We should look forward to heaven with eager anticipation. St. Paul, who had suffered a great deal, tells us that our present sufferings are as nothing compared to the glory that will be revealed in us (Rom 8:18). Our present life is necessarily hard; it does not mete out good for the deserving and evil for the rest in an arithmetically exact manner—far from it. But its inequalities will be smoothed out and justice restored in the future.

6 The future hope was an important part of St. Paul's daily life and also to our Methodist forefathers who, as Mr. Wesley said, "died well." The reason for this was that they felt that their earthly home was not a permanent house, just a temporary dwelling like the tent of a nomad. And they looked forward to a permanent dwelling, a house not made by hands, eternal in the heavens, a city founded by God (Heb 11). The hymn "Forever with the Lord" was commonly sung in the memorial service for old Methodist ministers who had striven and battled mightily for their Lord, which catches St. Paul's meaning well:

> Forever with the Lord. Amen so let it be
> Life from the dead is in that word 'tis immortality
> Here in the body pent absent from Him I roam
> But nightly pitch my moving tent a day's march nearer home.

7 We need to recapture this forward-looking spirit. If we only have hope in this life, we are of all men most miserable (1 Cor 15:19), but if we have in mind this great hope, we live and die better. It is not a case of abandoning our life and duties here and thinking only of heaven ("pie in the sky when you die"). We labor better and live better and die better when we know that our labor is not in vain but will be significant not only in this life but in the future, including our own life to come. Few people have been more heavenly minded than John Wesley ("one thing I want to know, the way to heaven"), but few people have striven more to make things better in the England of his time and indeed elsewhere as well.

8 Jesus told us in the parable about the rich fool to lay up our treasure in heaven, where moth and rust do not corrupt nor thieves break through and steal (Luke 12:13-21).

The First Letter of Peter

1 Peter 1:1-9

Peter, an apostle of Jesus Christ,

To God's elect, exiles scattered throughout the provinces of Pontus, Galatia, Cappadocia, Asia and Bithynia, who have been chosen according to the foreknowledge of God the Father, through the sanctifying work of the Spirit, to be obedient to Jesus Christ and sprinkled with his blood:

Grace and peace be yours in abundance.

Praise be to the God and Father of our Lord Jesus Christ! In his great mercy he has given us new birth into a living hope through the resurrection of Jesus Christ from the dead, and into an inheritance that can never perish, spoil or fade. This inheritance is kept in heaven for you, who through faith are shielded by God's power until the coming of the salvation that is ready to be revealed in the last time. In all this you greatly rejoice, though now for a little while you may have had to suffer grief in all kinds of trials. These have come so that the proven genuineness of your faith—of greater worth than gold, which perishes even though refined by fire—may result in praise, glory and honor when Jesus Christ is revealed. Though you have not seen him, you love him; and even though you do not see him now, you believe in him and are filled with an inexpressible and glorious joy, for you are receiving the end result of your faith, the salvation of your souls.

Comment

1 Peter was commanded by Christ to strengthen his brethren and to look after them as a shepherd minds his sheep, which on the day of Pentecost and thereafter he did and did it well. Non-Catholics note that there is no mention here

of any transfer of this function to any successors, much less that such successors would be the bishops of Rome.

2 With regard to the authorship of this letter, scholars are divided. Some favor the apostle Peter as the author; others argue for somebody else, perhaps a close associate of Peter. Arguments for and against ancient authorship all face several serious problems, especially those based on literary style. It was common for letter writers in those times to walk up and down dictating their letters to an amanuensis. The helper in this case was Sylvanus (Silas), who also worked with St. Paul and seems to have had some literary accomplishments. The authors did not literally dictate but rolled off a sentence or a paragraph and allowed the amanuensis to write it down as seemed best to them. A great deal of license was allowed to the scribe, so letters by the same author on different occasions might exhibit variations of style and phrasing. I have thought it best to go with the authorship claimed by the writer (surely one arguing so plainly and so righteously should not readily be taken to be a liar) and accept that these letters were authored (I did not say written) by the great apostle.

3 The context of the letter is persecution, again a difficult matter to pin down, as persecutions tended to be local in many cases and even the great ones varied in severity from place to place. Peter's advice would be the same to Christians suffering now, where persecutions still vary in type and severity from place to place. He would tell us that we may take a way of escape if that is available but, whatever happens, to be firm in our loyalty to Christ. Perhaps just as important, we must be careful how we live our lives so that we can silence the slanders of our detractors.

4 Finally, as in the rest of the Bible, we are encouraged to look beyond our present troubles and sufferings and rejoice for at least three reasons: first, it confirms that we are followers of Christ, who himself suffered unjustly, and his faithful followers should expect the same in some degree or other; second, the suffering is but for a little time on the earth with a great reward to follow; third, God will use it to do us good (like the refining of silver and gold); finally, it is an opportunity to commend our faith to the outsiders, for the blood of the martyrs is the seed of the church. St. Paul, when he was minding the clothes of the murderers, was probably struck by the example of Stephen, praying for those stoning him.

Highlights in the Epistle of James

The Epistle of James has so many valuable little jewels scattered here and there that it cannot readily be represented by a single or even a couple longer quotations. It is more like a load of buckshot than single, separate rifle discharges. Accordingly, we will list here the sort of things he said with the citations for them and perhaps a brief comment here and there. The best advice we can give to anyone about this little book is to read it. It is quite short.

Consider it pure joy, my brothers and sisters, whenever you face trials of many kinds, because you know that the testing of your faith produces perseverance (1:2-3).

If any of you lacks wisdom, you should ask God, who gives generously to all without finding fault, and it will be given to you (1:5).

Believers in humble circumstances ought to take pride in their high position. But the rich should take pride in their humiliation—since they will pass away like a wild flower (1:9-10).

When tempted, no one should say, "God is tempting me." For God cannot be tempted by evil, nor does he tempt anyone; but each person is tempted when they are dragged away by their own evil desire and enticed (1:13-14).

Everyone should be quick to listen, slow to speak and slow to become angry, because human anger does not produce the righteousness that God desires (1:19-20).

Those who consider themselves religious and yet do not keep a tight rein on their tongues deceive themselves, and their religion is worthless (1:26). [James has much to say about controlling our tongues.]

My brothers and sisters, believers in our glorious Lord Jesus Christ must not show favoritism (2:1). [James continues through v. 13 with his warning about paying more attention to rich or important people than to those who are poor and "unimportant."]

Faith by itself, if it is not accompanied by action, is dead…. Show me your faith without deeds, and I will show you my faith by my deeds (2:17, 18; continues through to v. 26).

Who is wise and understanding among you? But the wisdom that comes from heaven is first of all pure; then peace-loving, considerate, submissive, full of mercy and good fruit, impartial and sincere (3:13, 17).

Resist the devil, and he will flee from you (4:7).

Now listen, you who say, "Today or tomorrow we will go to this or that city, spend a year there, carry on business and make money." Why, you do not even know what will happen tomorrow. What is your life? You are a mist that appears for a little while and then vanishes. Instead, you ought to say, "If it is the Lord's will, we will live and do this or that" (4:13-15).

Is anyone among you in trouble? Let them pray. Is anyone happy? Let them sing songs of praise. Is anyone among you sick? Let them call the elders of the church to pray over them and anoint them with oil in the name of the Lord. And the prayer offered in faith will make the sick person well; the Lord will raise them up. If they have sinned, they will be forgiven (5:13-15).

Comment

1 This letter from James, the Lord's brother (not the apostle who was killed by Herod in order to please the Jews), is not easy to discuss as it consists of lots of little pieces that are valuable but require little commentary. The ones concerning the tongue are notable and apt, but the others are likewise timely.

2 The final exhortation may seem a little strange to our generation. We are accustomed to sophisticated medical diagnostics and treatments, but in the ancient world medical science was nonexistent, so they did what they could and relied on prayer for the rest. Jesus anointed the blind man's eyes with clay moistened by saliva, which was a common treatment for eye infections, and then healed them by spiritual means. With so much effective medical help, we sometimes forget or ignore spiritual means. The sensible thing is to use such medical means as are available and then to pray in faith.

3 This does not mean that the blind will see and the lame walk as in the days of Christ (these were signs of the coming of the Messiah), but the prayer of faith does make a difference. Patients who are prayed for do better (ask any hospital chaplain), and there are statistical studies to the same effect. Remarkable cures, especially of terminal cancers, quite commonly follow prayer (I know of two cases in the past few months where the patient was already admitted to hospice for terminal care). Every story is not so dramatic, of course; such miraculous inter-

ventions every time we prayed would lead to a topsy-turvy world. But God never sends us away empty-handed.

4 We should believe that our prayers are always answered even if they do not result in spectacular miracles on the spot. Some gift is given to the patient and to their family, and often a great peace comes to them with an assurance that God is with them and will bless them in some unexpected ways.

The First Epistle of John

1 John 2:1-11

My dear children, I write this to you so that you will not sin. But if anybody does sin, we have an advocate with the Father—Jesus Christ, the Righteous One. He is the atoning sacrifice for our sins, and not only for ours but also for the sins of the whole world.

We know that we have come to know him if we keep his commands. Whoever says, "I know him," but does not do what he commands is a liar, and the truth is not in that person. But if anyone obeys his word, love for God is truly made complete in them. This is how we know we are in him: Whoever claims to live in him must live as Jesus did.

Dear friends, I am not writing you a new command but an old one, which you have had since the beginning. This old command is the message you have heard. Yet I am writing you a new command; its truth is seen in him and in you, because the darkness is passing and the true light is already shining.

Anyone who claims to be in the light but hates a brother or sister is still in the darkness. Anyone who loves their brother and sister lives in the light, and there is nothing in them to make them stumble. But anyone who hates a brother or sister is in the darkness and walks around in the darkness. They do not know where they are going, because the darkness has blinded them.

Comment

1 The marked similarity between the language and ideas of John's Gospel and those in the three Johannine epistles supports the almost universal view that they are from the same hand. John, together with Mary the mother of Jesus, whose care he had assumed at Jesus' word to him from the cross, reportedly went to live in Ephesus and died there at a great age. The letters are generally thought to have been written in his later years. The Johannine authorship of the letters is disputed by some for no sound reasons (minor differences in language and phrasing).

2 The major themes of the letters follow those of the Gospel: darkness and light; showing love by keeping the commandments of Jesus: the vital command is to believe in the one God has sent and turn our lives over to him; the new com-

mandment is to love one another. All of these themes serve to identify the writer of the letters as the evangelist.

3 The two commandments, especially the first one—to walk as he walked—seem to put the bar impossibly high. But we are not expected to walk exactly and literally as Jesus walked; that would make us divine. But Jesus was meek and unselfish, walking with God, doing good, and showing concern about each of the flawed human beings he encountered. As we have truly opened our hearts to him, we seek to live along these lines with the power of the Holy Spirit to guide and help us. So by walking with him, even as fallible human beings, we are surely walking as he walked.

4 All three letters should be read (they are not very long). For all three (as Lord Bacon recommended for good books) read, mark, learn, and inwardly digest them.

Revelation 1

I, John, your brother and companion in the suffering and kingdom and patient endurance that are ours in Jesus, was on the island of Patmos because of the word of God and the testimony of Jesus. On the Lord's Day I was in the Spirit, and I heard behind me a loud voice like a trumpet, which said: "Write on a scroll what you see and send it to the seven churches: to Ephesus, Smyrna, Pergamum, Thyatira, Sardis, Philadelphia and Laodicea."

I turned around to see the voice that was speaking to me. And when I turned I saw seven golden lampstands, and among the lampstands was someone like a son of man, dressed in a robe reaching down to his feet and with a golden sash around his chest. The hair on his head was white like wool, as white as snow, and his eyes were like blazing fire. His feet were like bronze glowing in a furnace, and his voice was like the sound of rushing waters. In his right hand he held seven stars, and coming out of his mouth was a sharp, double-edged sword. His face was like the sun shining in all its brilliance.

When I saw him, I fell at his feet as though dead. Then he placed his right hand on me and said: "Do not be afraid. I am the First and the Last. I am the Living One; I was dead, and now look, I am alive for ever and ever! And I hold the keys of death and Hades.

"Write, therefore, what you have seen, what is now and what will take place later. The mystery of the seven stars that you saw in my right hand and of the seven golden lampstands is this: The seven stars are the angels of the seven churches, and the seven lampstands are the seven churches. (vv. 9-20)

Comment

1 The book of Revelation (Apocalypse) is notoriously difficult to understand. It is the only book in the Bible on which the great John Calvin did not write a commentary (he said he could not understand a word of it). It almost sounds like the ravings of someone tortured out of their wits. Yet the poet Samuel Taylor Coleridge declared that it was the most carefully contrived work he had ever seen. And he was right. Every part is lucid and meaningful once you understand the

message it carried to the beleaguered churches in Asia Minor during the persecutions of the late first century. Indeed, it is the crowning piece of the New Testament, which ties everything together, spelling out the future so that we would be able to meet it. Some parts of it are not so difficult to understand, and even the more difficult passages carry an important message to us today. William Barkley's two-volume commentary on the Apocalypse is helpful in providing further explanation of the imagery in the book.

2 The Apocalypse is unanimously ascribed by the ancients to the Apostle John, and though the genre is quite different, there are enough marked similarities in the thinking to make the Johannine authorship believable.

3 The island of Patmos lies in the eastern Mediterranean off the coast of Turkey, and it was one of the places to which the Romans sent political prisoners and other undesirables. It is about twelve miles long and ten across at its widest part (north). It is very rocky with a good harbor and has a population today of around 3,000. Christians fleeing from the Turks used to go there, and there is a sizable monastery on the top of a mountain. John is believed to have been exiled there around AD 95 and allowed home to Ephesus about a year later. The cave where John was allegedly chained up at night is still shown to visitors. Those imprisoned for serious crimes, like refusing to sacrifice to the emperor, might be subject to hard labor and confinement.

4 John, in the Spirit on the Lord's day, heard a voice, and when he turned to see who was speaking, he saw one like the Son of Man, who was clearly the risen Christ (I was dead and am alive again). The seven candlesticks are the seven churches in the province of Asia, and the seven stars are their angels (sometimes that imagery is used of the bishops caring for a church). He had a sword, but it was in his mouth, so his warfare was not military but waged by his word. The overall message of this vision is plain and important. The struggling infant churches were facing the might of a hostile Roman Empire. This vision is reminding them that God, in the person of Christ, is still in charge. Christ is the Alpha and Omega (the first and last letters in the Greek alphabet). He works quietly but effectively, bringing down empires and powers and supporting his little flock. We need to remember this today when we are opposed by mighty forces and powerful organizations. We should be confident of the future, for God has the last word.

5 The imagery of the hair (white like wool) is used to describe God and implies the divinity of Christ. The feet and footwear were typical of the Roman soldier who could march anywhere and tread down resistance. The feet or footwear here is of brass much more powerful than the boots of the Roman legions.

6 The seven churches were in a ring of cities that formed a postal route in the Roman province of Asia. John would no doubt have traveled that route looking after the churches there. He was obviously well acquainted with the peculiar circumstances of each of these cities, and this knowledge shows in the messages to the churches there.

To the Church in Ephesus

Revelation 2:1-7

To the angel of the church in Ephesus write:

These are the words of him who holds the seven stars in his right hand and walks among the seven golden lampstands. I know your deeds, your hard work and your perseverance. I know that you cannot tolerate wicked people, that you have tested those who claim to be apostles but are not, and have found them false. You have persevered and have endured hardships for my name, and have not grown weary.

Yet I hold this against you: You have forsaken the love you had at first. Consider how far you have fallen! Repent and do the things you did at first. If you do not repent, I will come to you and remove your lampstand from its place. But you have this in your favor: You hate the practices of the Nicolaitans, which I also hate.

Whoever has ears, let them hear what the Spirit says to the churches. To the one who is victorious, I will give the right to eat from the tree of life, which is in the paradise of God.

Comment

1 The church in Ephesus was a strong church that had battled successfully for the faith on several fronts. It had weeded out the heretical teachers and false apostles and persevered and borne hardship for the faith. Not many could say as much. But they had lost their first love; they had become a successful and reputable business. This is a serious problem in all institutions. Zeal and vision produce success, and the institution then focuses on maintaining itself instead of keeping in mind the beliefs and practices that produced it. This human tendency is deadly in the church. Tradition takes over from live faith, and slow death follows.

2 One of the first signs of this is divisions among the members. When the flame of love dies in a church, disputes and parties inevitably appear, and they are deadly.

3 John advises them (and us) to return to our first love, and he promises us that when we do so, we will eat from the tree of life. In the Genesis story the fruit

of this tree gave eternal life. This may and indeed does refer to heaven, but since eternal life begins here on earth, it can also mean that our spiritual life will be enriched and our spiritual nature refreshed so that we can go forward with God again in a real and live partnership—not just working *for* God but working *with* God. Being eternal, this progress cannot be blocked by any earthly power.

To the Church in Smyrna

To the angel of the church in Smyrna write:

These are the words of him who is the First and the Last, who died and came to life again. I know your afflictions and your poverty—yet you are rich! I know about the slander of those who say they are Jews and are not, but are a synagogue of Satan. Do not be afraid of what you are about to suffer. I tell you, the devil will put some of you in prison to test you, and you will suffer persecution for ten days. Be faithful, even to the point of death, and I will give you life as your victor's crown.

Whoever has ears, let them hear what the Spirit says to the churches. The one who is victorious will not be hurt at all by the second death.

Comment

1 There are two sites for the ancient city of Smyrna. The older one was an Aeolian settlement, and the newer one was allegedly founded by Alexander the Great. This more recent city is the one mentioned in the Apocalypse. Smyrna was a beautiful city. Above the harbor rose Mount Pagos, which had a ring of beautiful temples shining with gold in the sun. This was known as the crown of Smyrna, and it features in the letter. The church in Smyrna was a poor church but spiritually rich. It was also a suffering church. It was being harassed and persecuted, in particular by Jews. We know from the Acts of the Apostles that Jews in the province of Asia stirred up mobs and made trouble for Paul so that he had to be smuggled out of the city on occasion to escape plots on his life. The saintly Polycarp, bishop of Smyrna, was burned alive at the stake in AD 160, largely at the instigation of Jews, who even carried wood on the Sabbath day for the fire. John says that these are not "real" Jews, meaning they are not children of Abraham. He even says that they belong to the synagogue of Satan.

2 He warns the church in Smyrna that they will face persecution for a time and that some of them, like Polycarp, will die. But the promise to them is that they will receive the crown of life from Jesus. St. Paul told us that if we suffer with him, we shall also reign with him (2 Tim 2:12). And don't forget that Jesus told us to rejoice when we are persecuted, for we know then that we are in the right company.

3 Few of us, if any, in this country will be hauled into court for being Christians, but we can expect to be ridiculed and sneered at, perhaps overlooked for promotion and picked on in other small ways. Paul would tell us, "Do not be overcome by evil, but overcome evil with good" (Rom 12:21).

To the Church in Pergamum

Revelation 2:12-17

altar at Pergamon

To the angel of the church in Pergamum write:

These are the words of him who has the sharp, double-edged sword. I know where you live—where Satan has his throne. Yet you remain true to my name. You did not renounce your faith in me, not even in the days of Antipas, my faithful witness, who was put to death in your city—where Satan lives.

Nevertheless, I have a few things against you: There are some among you who hold to the teaching of Balaam, who taught Balak to entice the Israelites to sin so that they ate food sacrificed to idols and committed sexual immorality. Likewise, you also have those who hold to the teaching of the Nicolaitans. Repent therefore! Otherwise, I will soon come to you and will fight against them with the sword of my mouth.

Whoever has ears, let them hear what the Spirit says to the churches. To the one who is victorious, I will give some of the hidden manna. I will also give that person a white stone with a new name written on it, known only to the one who receives it.

Comment

1 This letter is full of references to the state of things in Pergamum. This city was the center for several kinds of pagan worship. There was a huge altar to Apollo overlooking the city and many other temples that might be considered Satan's throne. But probably the reference here is to the fact that Pergamum was the center of emperor-worship. Pergamum was a city loyal to Rome and had early applied for permission to build a temple for emperor-worship, and enforcing this practice throughout the province of Asia was part of their task.

2 The church in Pergamum had not yielded to these pressures and even had one martyr, Antipas, who may have been their bishop. They had held fast to the faith in Jesus Christ, as we must, for it is not for sale and cannot be negotiated away. This is what makes any congregation part of the holy catholic (meaning "worldwide") church.

3 They had a few bad entries in their account book. They were tolerating in their midst certain teachers and people who were following the way of Balaam in the book of Numbers, who for gain had encouraged the Moabite women to seduce the Israelites so that they joined them in idolatry and sexual immorality (closely related to one another). These Balaamites, as we may call them, seem to have been much the same as the Nicolaitans, who supposedly took their name

from Nicolas the proselyte of Antioch, the deacon, who in his later years was said to have fallen away and become heretical and immoral. Christian standards of behavior include not only fundamental tenets of faith but also practice. Those who follow Christ should walk as he walked (1 John). The church in Pergamum is commanded to repent or Christ will come and war against them with the sword of his mouth. God's truth is a mighty weapon.

4 The reference to the sword in the mouth of Christ reflects the Roman practice of giving to certain magistrates the power of life and death, which was called the *jus gladii* ("the right to use the sword"). Christ's sword is in his mouth, in his words, sharper and more powerful than any two-edged sword.

5 These things are promised to those who overcome: (1) Hidden manna: A jar of manna was kept in the ark of the covenant, later removed to a place of safety, possibly in Ethiopia. This promise would probably refer to a place at the messianic feast. (2) A white stone with a name on it: A stone was a frequent gift with religious significance among Jews. The name would be either the name of Christ or, more likely, the new name that was given to converts on baptism—their Christian name, given to witness that they were a new person, a child of the promise.

The Dead Church at Sardis

Revelation 3:1-6

To the angel of the church in Sardis write:

These are the words of him who holds the seven spirits of God and the seven stars. I know your deeds; you have a reputation of being alive, but you are dead. Wake up! Strengthen what remains and is about to die, for I have found your deeds unfinished in the sight of my God. Remember, therefore, what you have received and heard; hold it fast, and repent. But if you do not wake up, I will come like a thief, and you will not know at what time I will come to you.

Yet you have a few people in Sardis who have not soiled their clothes. They will walk with me, dressed in white, for they are worthy. The one who is victorious will, like them, be dressed in white. I will never blot out the name of that person from the book of life, but will acknowledge that name before my Father and his angels. Whoever has ears, let them hear what the Spirit says to the churches.

Comment

1 Sardis was the capital of the old kingdom of Lydia, which had prospered under Roman rule and become a center of trade and fabric manufacture. It had the trade guilds that went along with this kind of commercial activity and all the moral laxity that pervaded it. It was reportedly an extremely sinful city, and the Christian church there, though apparently functioning successfully, had very little real worship or growth or Christian activity going on in it and was therefore, though seemingly alive, in fact dead. The city of Sardis was in an almost impregnable position, with high cliffs on all sides, but it had twice been taken and sacked due to overconfidence and failure to keep a careful watch. These episodes were used in this letter to warn the church in Sardis not to repeat this serious mistake.

2 This leads us to ask, "What is a live church?" Sometimes it is taken to be a lively, well-attended church with large numbers of members, busy and well-staffed youth activities, and strong financially. But these features do not describe what Christ wants from a body of people that bears his name.

3 An important question to ask about a church is whether there is faith in it—not only the unchanging apostolic faith but also the manner in which it is held, personal faith and commitment to Christ well represented among the members.

4 Another important question is whether there is prayer going on in the church—not only the prayers that are part of the services on Sunday but with members individually and in groups engaging in prayer for Christ's work of every kind. Prayer ensures that we are not just working *for* Christ but working *with* him under his guidance and blessing. Remember how Jesus prayed and taught us to pray.

5 We also need to ask whether there is Christian mercy being shown in the church for people in need and trouble of every kind, both local and worldwide.

6 Another important question is whether there is outreach in the church—seeking to spread the message of Christ and win others for his kingdom.

7 .Finally, there is the question of whether there is growth in the church and not just growth in membership. We are intended individually and together to grow in grace and in the knowledge of Jesus Christ. The study of the Bible is a vital part of the Christian life and also of church life. Is there a weekly meeting for Bible study in the church, and how is it attended and valued? If there is not, we need to ask why not. Do groups of concerned people meet during the week for prayer? Great revivals of religion commonly originate in such groups of prayerful people.

8 If the answers to all these questions are depressing, we are encouraged by the letter to Sardis not to give up and retire. Even in this moribund church there was some life, and there always is. So long as the name of Christ remains in a body, there is hope. The prophet Isaiah said of God that he would not break the bruised staff nor snuff out the dimly burning torch (Isa 42:3). So those members who still care should waken up, pray, and get busy, expecting the Lord to work with them to breathe life into the corpse and make it once again a live church. Remember also the valley of dry bones in Ezekiel that the word of God made alive again to become a vast army.

Letter to the Church in Thyatira

Revelation 2:18-29

To the angel of the church in Thyatira write:

These are the words of the Son of God, whose eyes are like blazing fire and whose feet are like burnished bronze. I know your deeds, your love and faith, your service and perseverance, and that you are now doing more than you did at first.

Nevertheless, I have this against you: You tolerate that woman Jezebel, who calls herself a prophet. By her teaching she misleads my servants into

sexual immorality and the eating of food sacrificed to idols. I have given her time to repent of her immorality, but she is unwilling. So I will cast her on a bed of suffering, and I will make those who commit adultery with her suffer intensely, unless they repent of her ways. I will strike her children dead. Then all the churches will know that I am he who searches hearts and minds, and I will repay each of you according to your deeds.

Now I say to the rest of you in Thyatira, to you who do not hold to her teaching and have not learned Satan's so-called deep secrets, "I will not impose any other burden on you, except to hold on to what you have until I come."

To the one who is victorious and does my will to the end, I will give authority over the nations—that one "will rule them with an iron scepter and will dash them to pieces like pottery"—just as I have received authority from my Father. I will also give that one the morning star. Whoever has ears, let them hear what the Spirit says to the churches.

Comment

1 The inscription to the letter referring to Christ as the Son of God is unique in the Apocalypse, and it is thought that, along with some other statements about fire in the addressing of the letter, it refers to the three faithful Israelites in the fiery furnace in the book of Daniel, who were accompanied in their trial by one like unto the son of God.

2 Thyatira was the smallest and least important of the seven cities addressed in the Apocalypse. It was an important commercial city noted for its manufacturing, especially fabrics, and they had a special and expensive purple dye. The workers were organized into specialty trade guilds so that it was impossible to earn a living unless you were a member of a guild. This posed a problem for Christians since pagan religious rituals were involved in guild membership and also feasts that employed meats that had been sacrificed to idols and were then sold in the meat market. Drunkenness and sexual immorality were common accompaniments of these rituals. The danger was for Christians to close their eyes to what was going on and participate in the guilds on the principle that "business is business." The problem, of course, is that you can't hang around with pigs and not get dirty.

3 The woman who was encouraging all this was named Jezebel in the letter, after Queen Jezebel in 1 Kings, who led her husband, Ahab, and Israel into the same kind of thing with Baal-worship. This church member appears to have been arrogant and to have scorned reproof, even considering her views as more enlightened and holding that she was possessed of a deeper wisdom than that of the ordinary church members. It may even be that she operated a house church associated with the main body of believers.

4 The main body of Christians in Thyatira were praiseworthy. It was especially good that they were going forward and progressing, not standing still on their laurels or, worse, backsliding. They were praiseworthy also in that they did not approve or follow the teachings of this Jezebel, but they tolerated her and perhaps were afraid to confront her (as Ahab and even Elijah were). This would be a danger to the less mature Christians and young Christians generally, especially with the lure of prosperity as participating guild members.

5 The same kind of temptation exists even in lands where persecution is less obvious. A person can compromise his or her Christian integrity in order to fit in better in the world of business or politics, and it is equally dangerous. We

must put on the whole armor of God, let it be known whose we are, and above all else stand firm.

6 John counseled the church in Thyatira to hold fast to what was good, promising them several rewards. They were first promised that they would prevail and rule the nations. This is hardly intended in a literal sense, but the faithful do overcome and prevail in the end; the meek inherit the earth: "Crowns and thrones may perish, kingdoms rise and wane, but the church of Jesus constant will remain" (from the hymn "Onward, Christian Soldiers"). This has happened many times in the past and will continue to happen. The godless empires eventually crumble and disintegrate. When we are faithful to God, he will lead us to triumph, not in the earthly sense of taking over the government, though it has earthly consequences. The strong secular forces pressing on our society will ultimately, one by one, fail and fade, and the meek shall inherit the earth (Matt 5:5).

7 The promise of the morning star has proved puzzling to commentators, and several interpretations have been put forward for it, but in the main it is taken to refer to Christ himself. The greatest reward that any church or individual can ask for is the presence of Christ in their hearts and lives.

The Open-door Church at Philadelphia

Revelation 3:7-13

To the angel of the church in Philadelphia write:

These are the words of him who is holy and true, who holds the key of David. What he opens no one can shut, and what he shuts no one can open. I know your deeds. See, I have placed before you an open door that no one can shut. I know that you have little strength, yet you

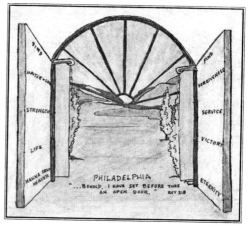

have kept my word and have not denied my name. I will make those who are of the synagogue of Satan, who claim to be Jews though they are not, but are liars—I will make them come and fall down at your feet and acknowledge that I have loved you. Since you have kept my command to endure patiently, I will also keep you from the hour of trial that is going to come on the whole world to test the inhabitants of the earth.

I am coming soon. Hold on to what you have, so that no one will take your crown. The one who is victorious I will make a pillar in the temple of my God. Never again will they leave it. I will write on them the name of my God and the name of the city of my God, the new Jerusalem, which is coming down out of heaven from my God; and I will also write on them my new name. Whoever has ears, let them hear what the Spirit says to the churches.

Comment

1 Philadelphia lay at the mouth of the river Hormus at a crossroads linking it to several other centers. The main trade road, from west to east, runs through the mountains so that it is indeed the door to the Middle East. It was a prosperous city, in particular noted for its wine industry, which led to the worship of Dionysus, the god of wine and fertility, whose rituals were drunken orgies accompanied by gross immorality. There was a large Jewish population in Philadelphia that, like

the Jews in Anatolia generally, persecuted the smaller Christian population. The area was also subject to serious earthquakes, and the city was completely destroyed by a major quake in AD 17 but completely rebuilt through the generosity of the Roman emperor. The citizens of the city were most grateful and loyal to Rome. Philadelphia became a major center of emperor-worship and considered themselves to be Roman allies if not citizens.

2 The letter to the Philadelphians reflects all these things. Christ opens a gateway that none shall close (see Isa 22:22); the Roman emperor was described by his worshipers as the holy one; Christ is described as the one who is holy and true (truly holy); the hostile Jews, it is said, will bow down before the Christians and acknowledge that they are the beloved of God; the faithful Christians of Philadelphia will be citizens of a greater city than Rome, the New Jerusalem; it will be a permanent honor—they will never be expelled as the Jews were from Rome. They will stand like temple pillars that will not be shaken (as by earthquakes).

3 The church in Philadelphia was uniformly praised for its firm stand for Christ against all the enemies of the cross, both heathen and Jewish. The only instruction given to it was to stand fast, lest someone steal their crown. This verse and many others are troublesome to the advocates of "once saved, always saved" but much commended by evangelical Arminians such as the Wesleys. Strict Calvinists can explain away all these verses in some sort or other, but it is probably simpler and better to take them at their face value and be watchful as the original Philadelphians failed to do and so lost their city.

4 The main message to the churches of the present is to beware of complacency. The church must sail on the water of society, not tuck itself away in some safe harbor, but it must not allow the water to leak into the ship. Above all they must be true to King Jesus through thick and thin. Their sure reward is to emerge victorious in this life (the meek inheriting the earth) and to receive the crown of glory in the world to come.

The Lukewarm Church: The Letter to Laodicea

Revelation 3:14-22

To the angel of the church in Laodicea write:

These are the words of the Amen, the faithful and true witness, the ruler of God's creation. I know your deeds, that you are neither cold nor hot. I wish you were either one or the other! So, because you are lukewarm— neither hot nor cold—I am about to spit you out of my mouth. You say, "I am rich; I have acquired wealth and do not need a thing." But you do not realize that you are wretched, pitiful, poor, blind and naked. I counsel you to buy from me gold refined in the fire, so you can become rich; and white clothes to wear, so you can cover your shameful nakedness; and salve to put on your eyes, so you can see.

Those whom I love I rebuke and discipline. So be earnest and repent. Here I am! I stand at the door and knock. If anyone hears my voice and opens the door, I will come in and eat with that person, and they with me.

To the one who is victorious, I will give the right to sit with me on my throne, just as I was victorious and sat down with my Father on his throne. Whoever has ears, let them hear what the Spirit says to the churches."

Comment

1 As usual, this letter is replete with references to things as they were in this city. It was prosperous, famous for its purple cloth and the fine work of its goldsmiths. It was also a medical center specializing in eye complaints that were

common in the Middle East in those times; in particular, they had an eye salve that was in high demand.

2 The church in Laodicea was not heretical or immoral, yet they were useless because they were apathetic. As the letter says, they were neither cold nor hot but just lukewarm, and this was just as deadly as the false teaching and low living of some of the other churches who had fallen into the ways of their heathen neighbors. There may be an additional bit of relevant local background here: there was said to be a fountain beside the road into the city that promised the thirsty traveler a cool drink but produced only warm volcanic water with a horrible metallic taste that you had to spit out of your mouth.

3 But they thought well of themselves, considering themselves to be rich, well dressed, with good eyesight (thanks to their famous eye salve), and generally in good shape. Lukewarm Christians commonly consider themselves to be more enlightened and spiritually healthy than the rest. The message of the risen Christ, however, tells them that they would be better off to be either cold or hot and offers to spew them out of his mouth in disgust.

4 But even this self-satisfied lot are not altogether abandoned as being hopeless. They are counseled to buy of Christ pure gold in order to be truly rich, effective healing eye salve so that they could really see, and the white garments of true righteousness to cover their nakedness.

5 They are going to be chastened, but again hope is offered. The chastening of God is intended to lead to repentance and restoration.

6 Finally, the Laodiceans are informed that Christ, so far from altogether rejecting them, is knocking on their door. If anyone hears his voice and opens the door, he will come in, and it will be party time, like when the prodigal son returned home. Their candlestick will be restored to its place in Christ's kingdom, and they will inherit all the promises made by Christ to his church.

7 The messages of the Apocalypse reveal some pretty sick churches, but even the worst of them was not considered hopeless. It is true that, like the prodigal son, they must come to themselves and repent and seek the way back to their proper place with the Father. But Christ is ready to meet and restore them.

8 Holman Hunt's famous picture representing this letter shows Christ knocking at the door. And the painting has one very important feature: There is no handle on the outside; the door must be opened from the inside.

The Dragon and the Beast

Revelation 13

The dragon stood on the shore of the sea. And I saw a beast coming out of the sea. It had ten horns and seven heads, with ten crowns on its horns, and on each head a blasphemous name. The beast I saw resembled a leopard, but had feet like those of a bear and a mouth like that of a lion. The dragon gave the beast his power and his throne and great authority. One of the heads of the beast seemed to have had a fatal wound, but the fatal wound had been healed. The whole world was filled with wonder and followed the beast. People worshiped the dragon because he had given authority to the beast, and they also worshiped the beast and asked, "Who is like the beast? Who can wage war against it?"

The beast was given a mouth to utter proud words and blasphemies and to exercise its authority for forty-two months. It opened its mouth to blaspheme God, and to slander his name and his dwelling place and those who live in heaven. It was given power to wage war against God's holy people and to conquer them. And it was given authority over every tribe, people, language and nation. All inhabitants of the earth will worship the beast—all whose names have not been written in the Lamb's book of life, the Lamb who was slain from the creation of the world.

Whoever has ears, let them hear. (vv. 1-9)

Comment

1 More recent biblical scholars, such as R. H. Charles, have viewed Revelation as a species of symbolic writing similar to the book of Daniel. A number of such books were written in the intertestamental period. They tended to appear in times of great persecution and to have been a sort of secret writing that only the initiated could understand (he that has ears, let him hear). They are best understood as a form of parable.

2 The background of the Apocalypse was the Roman persecution of the church. The reason for this was because Christians refused to pour out a glass of wine as a sacrifice to the divine emperor. Most people had no trouble with this as they were then allowed to go on with their own religion without hindrance. But loyal Christians could not do it. Polycarp, bishop of Smyrna, was beloved by all, and

the Roman authorities begged him to pour out the ritual glass of wine; he could not do it: "These eighty and two years have I served him, nor has he ever done me any wrong. How could I now deny my Christ?"

3 The dragon is the devil, Lucifer the fallen angel, and he uses earthly agents to do his work. In this case the agent was the Roman government with the divine emperor at its head. This is the beast with numerous heads, corresponding to various emperors. The head that was wounded and returned to life has been identified with Nero, the mad emperor who was popularly believed to have survived and returned to life (*Nero redivivus*).

4 The beast was given power and authority by the dragon, and the whole earth worshiped the beast. This should not be taken literally. It is like Elijah's statement that he was the only one remaining true to God while there were 7,000 left who had never bowed the knee to Baal nor kissed his hand.

5 The beast has been identified confidently with various evil powers over the centuries since. Genghis Khan is one likely candidate, more modernly Hitler and his Nazis and then Stalin and the Communist menace. In the early Reformation movement and still in some conservative circles, the beast has been identified with the medieval Roman Catholic Church with the Pope as the antichrist. The Spanish Inquisition was similarly regarded as it attempted to stamp out by cruelty and force the return to the Bible of the Reformation.

6 None of these is a perfect fit, and perhaps it is better to identify the beast with any or all of those (and there have been many and no doubt will be more to come) who oppose the kingdom of Christ and war against the church. There are great beasts and lesser beasts, but there will always be some serious opposition, and if we try to live the Christian life as the Master taught us, we will surely find them, or they will surely find us.

7 We are not urged to fight against the beast. Christ and his angels will do that, and the beast will be cast down. Our duty is to persevere and be faithful, if need be unto death. Our principal weapon is prayer, and the prayers of the saints are made fragrant with incense and carried up to the throne of God in golden bowls (a most encouraging way to look at our prayers, which often seem to us cold and inadequate). They may not seem much as we offer them, but they improve greatly on the way up.

8 It is noticeable that in the Apocalypse, the defeated beast and the dragon keep reorganizing and returning to take up the battle afresh so that the struggle never ends. So when we have a victory over the evil one, we should not lay down our arms, for he will surely be back. This will go on until the final victory that presages the return of Christ and the establishment of his kingdom.

The New Jerusalem

Revelation 21

One of the seven angels who had the seven bowls full of the seven last plagues came and said to me, "Come, I will show you the bride, the wife of the Lamb."
(v. 1)

Read through verse 27 in your Bible.

Comment

1 The final chapters of the Apocalypse of John are the cap on the entirety of the Bible, the vision as to where everything is leading and how it will all be consummated. I have therefore quoted it at length.

2 Learned commentators have shied away from Revelation because it is mysterious, and it is often difficult to discern exactly what it means. It has also suffered much at the hands of unlearned commentators who have applied it confidently to current events and used it to predict the future in some detail. Some have used it to predict the precise date, and sometimes even the hour of the day, when the world would come to an end. These uniformly prove wrong, which is hardly surprising, for Jesus said, "Of that day and hour no one knows, not even the angels of heaven, nor the Son, but the Father alone" (Matt 24).

3 It is best, therefore, to remember once more what the great Dr. Beet has repeatedly advised us: to tread carefully and cautiously, remembering that prophecy and the fulfillment of prophecy are two very different things.

4 This vision is telling us that God will bring all things to fulfillment, putting an end to sin and wickedness and making all things new. We don't know whether this consummation will be in the material plane as we know it, in a spiritual dimension, or in a completely new heaven and earth. It is described to us in figurative terms; indicative speech could not do it justice and indeed would be nearly meaningless to us, like trying to match the terms of mathematical astrophysics with our everyday notions about the universe.

5 The heavenly Jerusalem is of unimaginable splendor and beauty. It is four square, the same in length, breadth, and height, which indicates mathematical perfection. The size of the city is strange, 1,500 miles in every dimension. If it

were taken literally, it would reach into the stratosphere. But what the figure is telling us is its immense majesty, beyond anything we can imagine. It also speaks to us of enormous beauty. The gates are each composed of a single huge pearl (the pearly gates of common parlance). The city itself is built of purest gold, and the foundations, normally rubble with us, are precious stones, all symbols of great beauty.

6 A river of life flows out of the city with the tree of life in it, bespeaking immortality. On either side of this stream are trees that produce fruit year-round, with leaves of healing power to wipe away all sin and strife.

7 It will be a world of unmingled happiness, no sorrow or tears or sighing. Trouble and distress are good in preparing us for heaven and making sure we are fit to be there. But in the new heaven and earth there is no need for tribulation and sorrow, and sighing will flee away.

8 Above all it will be the abode of God and the Lamb. There will be no temple there because worship will be direct in the presence of God, who will shine there in all his glory so that there will be no night there either.

9 We have a foretaste of heaven here on earth. To be heavenly minded isn't to be of no earthly use. Quite the contrary, the future gives meaning to the present and sustains us in hardship here. Present things and duties are not made less important by knowing their future end; rather, the future goal makes the present things more important. The doctrine of creation makes that clear. Earthly things are made by God and reflect the mind and hand of their maker. We are here then to look after them and, as stewards, will be held accountable for how we manage them. They are important.

10 The millennium, the thousand years of peace that are said to follow the return of Christ, has given rise to a great deal of controversy and speculation. There are three basic views: (1) *Postmillennialism* says it has already happened in the victory of the church in the early and middle ages; (2) *Premillennialism* says it is about to happen following the return of Christ; (3) *Amillenialism* says it is not a particular period but something that is continually happening.

11 How will we occupy ourselves in heaven? I am sure that even our most superlative expectations will be inadequate. I like the Salvation Army's description of heaven as "higher service." In short, we will be busy, but doing what? The Jews believed that every blade of grass and every child had its guardian angel. And these latter were very important, for they continually behold the face of God

(like being able to go into the president's office without knocking). Who knows what we will be busy doing? But like our work here below, it will be a form of worship.

CPSIA information can be obtained
at www.ICGtesting.com
Printed in the USA
FFOW02n1657230118
44689171-44683FF